ENGLISH NEXT

Starter A1

Teacher's Resource Book

Anne Preier
Stuart Vizard

Hueber Verlag

English NEXT

Student's Book
Myriam Fischer Callus
Gareth Hughes
Birgit Meerholz-Härle

Teacher's Resource Book
Anne Preier
Stuart Vizard

Das Werk und seine Teile sind urheberrechtlich geschützt.
Jede Verwertung in anderen als den gesetzlich zugelassenen
Fällen bedarf deshalb der vorherigen schriftlichen
Einwilligung des Verlags.

Hinweis zu § 52a UrhG: Weder das Werk noch seine Teile dürfen ohne
eine solche Einwilligung überspielt, gespeichert und in ein Netzwerk
eingespielt werden. Dies gilt auch für Intranets von Firmen und von Schulen
und sonstigen Bildungseinrichtungen.

3. 2. 1. | Die letzten Ziffern
2011 10 09 08 07 | bezeichnen Zahl und Jahr des Druckes.
Alle Drucke dieser Auflage können, da unverändert,
nebeneinander benutzt werden.
1. Auflage
© 2007 Hueber Verlag, 85737 Ismaning, Deutschland

Verlagsredaktion: Thomas Bennett-Long, Heike Birner, Hueber Verlag, Ismaning
Umschlaggestaltung: Alois Sigl, Hueber Verlag, Ismaning
Zeichnungen: Sina Scheller-Persenico, Zürich; Hemera Technologies Inc., Quebec
Layout/Satz/Herstellung: Büro Sieveking, München
Reproarbeiten: Lorenz & Zeller, Inning a.A.
Druck und Bindung: Ludwig Auer GmbH, Donauwörth
Printed in Germany
ISBN 978-3-19-072931-9

NEXT Table of Contents

Starter, Unit 1	AIM	FOCUS	CAN DO	
1 I know English! pairs/small groups, matching, vocabulary	to match words with pictures to put words in groups	international words cognates	can understand single words	9
2 Match me! groups, game, vocabulary	to win a game by matching nouns with the corresponding adjectives	countries and nationalities	can say where I'm from and ask others where they're from	11

Starter, Unit 2	AIM	FOCUS	CAN DO	
3 Sorry, wrong number small groups, game	to win a game by matching digits with the equivalent words	telephone numbers	can ask others for their telephone number and give my own	13
4 Family matters pairs/small groups, sentence building, reading	to describe family relationships by building sentences	family relationships	can talk about family using simple language	16

Starter, Unit 3	AIM	FOCUS	CAN DO	
5 Is it true? pairs & whole class, interview, speaking	to win a competition by making correct guesses about a person	3rd person singular "s" questions with *do* free time activities (dis)agreeing	can ask simple personal questions	18
6 Work hard, play harder whole class, interview, speaking	to interview classmates to find out what free time activities they do	questions with *do* short answers free time activities	can say what I do in my free time	20

Starter, Unit 4	AIM	FOCUS	CAN DO	
7 My dream workplace pairs, dictation, speaking	to dictate and draw the position of objects in a room	prepositions of place *there is/are* objects and furniture in a workplace	can describe my ideal workplace can say where things are in a room	22
8 Who in the world? whole class, interview, speaking	to interview classmates and report findings	questions with *do* 3rd person singular "s" workplace, lifestyle	can ask and answer simple personal questions	24

Starter, Unit 5	AIM	FOCUS	CAN DO	
9 Numbermania! pairs, quiz, speaking	to win points by answering quiz questions correctly	numbers from 21–100	can say and understand numbers from 21 to 100	26
10 This is my life whole class, information exchange, speaking	to complete a life line by gathering information	past simple tense a life history	can understand a short text that describes someone's life history in simple sentences	28

NEXT Table of Contents

Starter, Unit 6	AIM	FOCUS	CAN DO	
11 A holiday romance pairs, jigsaw text, reading	to put a text together by matching pictures and text	past tense verb forms	can understand a simple text about a holiday	31
12 Where's the word? pairs, game, vocabulary	to guess words that are hidden in a grid	numbers from 1–10 the alphabet vocabulary from unit 6 *Is there …?*		33

A1, Unit 1	AIM	FOCUS	CAN DO	
13 Find your partner whole class, role play, speaking	to find a partner by introducing yourself	present simple, *to be* names; nationalities meeting/greeting/introducing	*can introduce myself and others* *can say where I'm from*	35
14 Classroom English pairs/groups, matching, reading	to match sentence beginnings and endings to form classroom instructions	classroom instructions the imperative		37

A1, Unit 2	AIM	FOCUS	CAN DO	
15 Can you? whole class, survey, speaking	to gather information about what students can do	*can/can't* skills		39
16 Alphabingo whole class, game	to recognize letters of the alphabet	the alphabet		41

A1, Unit 3	AIM	FOCUS	CAN DO	
17 What's the word? pairs, word puzzle, vocabulary	to solve a word puzzle	unit vocabulary adverbs of frequency		43
18 Food and drink whole class, interview, speaking	to find out about the food likes and dislikes of classmates	food and drink	*can ask what someone likes to eat and drink* *can say what I like to eat and drink*	45

A1, Unit 4	AIM	FOCUS	CAN DO	
19 Jenny's day whole class, information exchange, speaking	to find out what someone does at a certain time of day	daily routines times of day	*can say the time* *can describe the daily routines of others*	47
20 Time Snap groups, game	to win a game by matching analogue and digital times	telling the time	*can say the time*	50

4

NEXT Table of Contents

A1, Unit 5	AIM	FOCUS	CAN DO	
21 **History Quiz** whole class, quiz, listening	to guess the names of famous dead people	simple past verbs life stories	can understand simple statements about someone's life history	52
22 **What was the weather like?** pairs, information gap, speaking	to find out what the weather was like at a certain time and place	weather words past simple questions with *was*	can describe yesterday's and today's weather in simple words	54

A1, Unit 6	AIM	FOCUS	CAN DO	
23 **What did you do in Paris?** whole class, information exchange, speaking	to complete a fictitious holiday by collecting activity cards	past simple questions with *did* holiday activities	can talk about a past holiday can name common holiday activities	56
24 **Questions, questions!** pairs, interview, speaking	to find out what students have in common by asking questions	*wh*-questions with the past simple		59

A1, Unit 7	AIM	FOCUS	CAN DO	
25 **Neighbours** pairs, information gap, writing/speaking	to describe contrasting pictures in order to make comparative sentences	describing people descriptive adjectives comparative adjective form	can describe what other people look like can compare things and people in simple sentences	61
26 **Who's who?** groups, information exchange, reading/listening	to work out the family relationships in family trees	family relationships comparisons	can describe family relationships can make simple sentences comparing people	64

A1, Unit 8	AIM	FOCUS	CAN DO	
27 **An ideal place to live** pairs, guessing, reading/speaking	to make correct guesses about another person	neighbourhoods furniture accommodations	can describe the area in which I live can answer questions and give simple information about accommodations	67
28 **Home sweet home** pairs, information gap, speaking	to find differences in two pictures by asking questions / describing	prepositions of place *there is/are – is there/are there?* furniture/objects in a living room	can describe where things are in a room	69

NEXT Table of Contents

A1, Unit 9	AIM	FOCUS	CAN DO	
29 Out on the town groups, board game, speaking	to win a game by reaching finish first to talk about personal free time activities	places of entertainment free time activities	*can say what I do and did in my free time*	71
30 Well, I never! groups/whole class, speculating/interviewing, speaking	to speculate about what others do to find out if groups make better guesses than individuals	present simple questions with *do, how often, how much/many* past simple questions with *did* – adverbs of frequency	*can say how often I do something* *can ask about free time activities* *can say what I usually do and what I did in my free time*	73

A1, Unit 10	AIM	FOCUS	CAN DO	
31 Getting there groups, game, vocabulary	to win a word game by finding original answers	types of transport descriptive adjectives		77
32 Out and about pairs, dictation, speaking	to give and understand directions	giving directions buildings in a town	*can give and understand simple directions*	79

A1, Unit 11	AIM	FOCUS	CAN DO	
33 Let's go out! whole class, interview, speaking	to find partners for free time activities	making suggestions and arrangements accepting and declining invitations	*can make suggestions for going out*	81
34 What are you doing on Friday night? whole class, role play, speaking	to compare what people usually do at the weekend with fictitious plans	present continuous for the future fixed arrangements routine activities	*can name some things people do after work* *can ask about others' plans and talk about these plans*	83

A1, Unit 12	AIM	FOCUS	CAN DO	
35 Body and Soul Bingo whole class, game, vocabulary	to win a Bingo game by matching words with their definitions	health/illness the body		86
36 A healthy life whole class, interview, speaking	to find kindred spirits in the classroom	healthy lifestyle	*can say how often I do things*	90

Flextras 92

NEXT

INTRODUCTION

This Resource Book for teachers provides 36 photocopiable communicative activities for learners with little or no prior knowledge initially. It has been designed to accompany the Hueber ENGLISH NEXT coursebook series at the Starter and A1 level but it can also be used to supplement any adult English course at this level. The book is clearly structured and consists of a Table of Contents, 36 one- or two-page activities with the corresponding Teacher's notes, as well as 4 pages of *Flextras,* i.e. short additional classroom activities.

Using the Teacher's Resource Book

The activities in this Resource Book are organised to correspond to the structure of the ENGLISH NEXT Starter and A1 coursebooks. There are two activities per coursebook unit for both ENGLISH NEXT Starter and A1, beginning with 12 activities for the 6 Starter units followed by 24 activities for the 12 A1 units.

To select the appropriate activity for a lesson, look at the Table of Contents: for each activity, you will find the corresponding coursebook unit in the first column of the contents table. The Table of Contents provides further information which will enable you to find an activity that suits your needs, e.g.

- the activity form
- the aims of the activity
- the language focus
- the "can-do's" based on the CEF "can-do" descriptors

There are a variety of activity forms in the book – activities for pairs, small groups or the whole class such as games, quizzes, role plays, interviews, surveys, information exchange, and jigsaw texts. All of the activities are designed to give students enjoyable practice involving vocabulary, grammar and functions and the four skills of speaking, listening, reading and writing. Because the time needed for an activity is dependent on many different factors, the times given in the book provide only a general guideline to aid classroom time management.

Each activity focuses on one or more of the following: a particular lexical field (e.g. holidays), a specific grammatical point, an area of functional language (e.g. meeting and greeting). The "can-do" statements listed in the Table of Contents and in the Teacher's notes are based on one or more of the "can-do" statements to be found at the end of each ENGLISH NEXT coursebook unit in the *Exploring my progress* section.

No special equipment is necessary to carry out the activities. Sometimes the activities have role cards or separate boxes of information which must be cut out along the dotted lines indicated. They can be copied onto card and/or laminated for durability before being cut up. It is best to store sets of cards in separate bags or envelopes.

The Teacher's notes

The Teacher's notes can be found before each activity sheet for easy access. The top half of the notes names the activity type, aims, focus, approximate timing, the corresponding unit of the NEXT coursebook, and the "can-do" statements. The bottom half of the notes gives clear instructions on how to prepare the activities before the lesson – as well as easy-to-follow, step-by-step guidance for carrying them out.

Where relevant, the Teacher's notes make suggestions for activities with a written result which can be included in learners' Language Portfolios. The European *Language Portfolio* contains a section entitled Dossier in which learners can collect examples of interesting texts and other forms of written work which they have produced. For more information on the Portfolio, see pp. 62–69 of the ENGLISH NEXT Starter *Companion* booklet, pp. 142–152 of the A1 *Companion* booklet, or the Hueber ENGLISH NEXT website at www.hueber.de/next/portfolio.

NEXT

The Flextras

At the back of this Resource Book there are several pages of suggestions for short (approximately 5–10 minute) activities. These are flexible extra activities which can be used by teachers as lead-ins to a new topic, as fillers or for extra practice of specific vocabulary and structures. They require little or no pre-class preparation.

Further resources for teachers

Each volume of ENGLISH NEXT has its own comprehensive *Teacher's Guide* with an introduction to the ENGLISH NEXT approach and extra ideas and suggestions for teaching. The **CD-ROMs** to the coursebooks contain self-study exercises for learners, but also contain chronological and alphabetical wordlists with audio recordings of the vocabulary which will be of use to teachers. For additional teaching resources, visit the ENGLISH NEXT website at www.hueber.de/next. In the section for teachers you will find photocopiable downloads as well as further useful information, such as additional information about the NEXT concept and, for example, details of teacher-training workshops in your area. To access the downloads for specific units, there is a web code for every unit which is given at the bottom of the Teacher's notes page in this Resource Book.

We hope that this range of material will help you to add variety and depth to your teaching with ENGLISH NEXT and enable you to respond to the differing needs of different groups of students.

Your NEXT Team

NEXT STARTER   Unit 1

Activity 1   I know English!

Teacher's notes	Activity	Focus
	pairs/small groups, matching, vocabulary	international words; cognates
15–20 minutes	**Aim** to match English words with pictures to put words into categories	**Can do** *I can understand single words.*

Preparation

Copy one activity sheet for every 2 to 4 students in the class. Cut out each separate word and picture card on the activity sheet and mix. Keep each set of cards in separate bags or envelopes.

Procedure

The aim of the activity is to show students how many words they already know or can understand in English because of the similarity with German. The activity has two phases: (1) to match the word and picture cards, and (2) to put the words into groups/categories.

1. Put students into pairs or groups of 3 or 4. Give them a set of 32 cards and ask them to match the words with the pictures. While they are doing this, walk around the classroom, helping out where necessary. Check results with the whole class.

2. When students have finished the first phase of the activity, ask them to group the words, i.e. to put them into categories, such as "things to eat". Allow them about 5–10 minutes to do this.

3. Ask pairs or students from each group to read out the words in their word groups. Help with pronunciation, where necessary. It is important to stress that although many words look alike, they are not necessarily pronounced the same in both languages.

4. You can then write headings for the different word groups on the board/OHP (= food, musical instruments, machines and free time activities). If your students grouped their words using other categories, then simply find other headings, as long as their groupings are plausible.

NEXT STARTER   Unit 1

Activity 1   I know English!

banana		spaghetti	
	melon		broccoli
computer		radio	
	TV		CD player
guitar		keyboard	
	saxophone		cello
opera		concert	
	film		musical

NEXT STARTER   Unit 1

Activity 2   Match me!

Teacher's notes	Activity group work, game, vocabulary	Focus countries and nationalities
15 – 20 minutes	Aim to win a game by matching nouns with the corresponding adjective forms	Can do *I can say where I'm from and ask others where they are from.*

Preparation

Copy one activity sheet for every 3 students in the class. For a **memory game**, cut out all 36 cards on the sheet. Put each set of cards into a separate envelope or bag. For a **domino game**, cut the activity sheet into 18 cards by cutting down the middle vertical line so that in each horizontal row you have two cards with a country on the left and a nationality on the right; e.g. *Germany/ Swiss*. Put each set of 18 cards into an envelope or bag.

Procedure

The aim of the activity is to review the vocabulary of countries and nationalities in a game format. There are two ways students can play the game:

Memory
Players try to turn up matching cards by remembering where they are. A match consists of a country card with its corresponding nationality card. The object of the game is to win the most "tricks" or pairs.

Put your students into groups of 3. It is no problem if there are 4 students in some groups. Ask them to shuffle the 36 cards and to place them face down in rows on the desk. The first player begins by turning up any two cards. If they have a trick (a country and a nationality that match), they can keep it and play again. If not, they turn the two cards face down again in the same place and it is the next player's turn. The winner is the student with the most tricks at the end of the game.

Domino
Put your students into groups of 3. Three is the ideal number for this game because then students each get the same number of cards. But if your class doesn't divide into threes, you will have to have two or three groups with 4 students.

1. Ask students to shuffle the domino cards and to place them face down in a pile on the desk. Each player should then take 6 cards. Ask students to write a letter of the alphabet on a piece of paper without showing the others in their group. The student in each group whose letter of the alphabet is closest to "Z" begins.

2. The first player begins by placing one of their domino cards face up onto the desk. The next player looks at his/her cards and adds to the card on the desk if they can. For example, if the first player places the card with *Germany/Swiss* on it, the next player can only play if they have a card with *German* (which they place on the left of the card on the desk, so that *German* and *Germany* are next to each other) or *Switzerland* (which they place on the right of the card on the desk so that *Swiss* and *Switzerland* are next to each other). Play then moves on to the next student and the procedure is repeated.

3. If a player can't play because they don't have any corresponding dominoes, they miss a turn and play moves on to the next student.

4. The winner is the first player to get rid of all of their domino cards.

NEXT STARTER Unit 1

Activity 2   Match me!

Hungary	German	Germany	Swiss
Switzerland	Austrian	Austria	Scottish
Scotland	Italian	Italy	Spanish
Spain	French	France	English
England	Irish	Ireland	Russian
Russia	Polish	Poland	Turkish
Turkey	Greek	Greece	Belgian
Belgium	American	America (the USA)	Slovenian
Slovenia	Canadian	Canada	Hungarian

NEXT STARTER   Unit 2

Activity 3   Sorry, wrong number

Teacher's notes	Activity small groups, game	Focus telephone numbers
15–20 minutes	Aim to win card tricks by matching telephone numbers written in words with the same numbers in digits	Can do *I can ask others for their telephone number and give my own.*

Preparation

Copy one activity sheet A and one activity sheet B for every 3 or 4 students in the class. Cut out the 23 cards and keep each set in a bag or envelope.

Procedure

This game is a variation of the familiar card game "Old Maid" or "Schwarzer Peter." The object of the game is to avoid ending up with the "Sorry, wrong number" card.

1. Tell the class that they are going to play a variation of the card game "Schwarzer Peter" involving telephone numbers. Ask if anyone knows this game and can explain the basic rules to the class in German. (**Note:** A deck of "Schwarzer Peter" cards consists of pairs of matching cards with the exception of the "Schwarzer Peter" card which has no "partner." Players take turns drawing cards from each others' hands and laying down tricks whenever possible until someone is left with the "Schwarzer Peter." That person is the loser.)

2. Explain (also in German if necessary) that in this version of the game **the loser is the person who ends up with the "Sorry, wrong number" card.** Each trick will consist of a card with a telephone number in digits and another card with the same number in words. Demonstrate on the board/OHP by writing a phone number in digits and eliciting the words for each digit from your students.

3. The object is to play until all the cards are out of the game except the wrong number card. To make tricks, there are two possibilities. As in the classic "Schwarzer Peter" game, students can simply take turns drawing a card from the hand of the player on their left, and putting tricks down on the table as they get them. Then the students are practising their receptive skills with numbers and the equivalent words.

4. If you want them to practise saying the numbers aloud, students should ask the player on their left *Can you give me the phone number (x)…?* Write this phrase on the board/OHP.

5. Put your students into groups of 3 or 4. Give each group a set of 23 cards. Ask them to shuffle and deal out all the cards. Players begin by putting down any tricks they have been dealt by chance.
Note: Students should always show the other players their tricks and the whole group must agree that they match.

6. Player A begins either by drawing a card from the player to his/her left (Player B) or by asking him/her *Can you give me the phone number …?* followed by one of the phone numbers on his/her cards. If Player B does not have the card Player A asks for, Player A must draw a card at random from Player B's hand. If Player A gets a trick, he/she lays it down on the desk and gets another turn. If he/she doesn't get a trick, Player A keeps hold of the cards and Player B gets a turn, repeating the procedure with Player C and so on. Since players get a new card from their neighbour's hand each time they play, cards keep circulating and the "Sorry, wrong number" card, as well.

7. The game continues as described in point 6. Once a player gets rid of all his/her cards, he/she drops out of the game, but continues to monitor the matching cards fellow players lay down. The game ends when the last player is left with the "Sorry, wrong number" card.

NEXT STARTER Unit 2

Activity 3   Sorry, wrong number!   Sheet A

four-oh-one two-oh-six-oh	401 20 60	five-seven-three oh-nine-two-oh	573 09 20
eight-three-nine two-six-oh-one	839 26 01	double nine-one six-eight-oh-two	991 68 02
four-three-nine six-one-two-four	439 61 24	double six-three two-one-two-oh	663 21 20

© 2007 Hueber Verlag · This sheet may be photocopied and used in class.

NEXT STARTER Unit 2

Activity 3   Sorry, wrong number!   Sheet B

double two-five four-one-oh-six	225 41 06	one-oh-three five-six-two-oh	103 56 20
three-oh-two six-eight-oh-five	302 68 05	seven-six-seven four-five-one-oh	767 45 10
eight-double six two-oh-two-five	866 20 25	Sorry, wrong number!	

© 2007 Hueber Verlag · This sheet may be photocopied and used in class.

NEXT STARTER   Unit 2

Activity 4   Family matters

Teacher's notes

Activity
pairwork/small groups, sentence building, reading

20–25 minutes

Aim
to describe a family by building sentences

Focus
family relationships

Can do
I can talk about a family in simple language.

Preparation

Make one copy of the activity sheet for every 2 to 4 students in your class. Cut along the central dotted line and give one copy of the family tree to each pair or group. Cut out the word cards individually, mix them up and distribute one set to each pair or group.

Procedure

The aim of this activity is to put together the word cards to make sentences which describe Mark's family.

1. Ask students to look at the family tree and explain that they are going to recreate a text which Mark has written about his family. Tell them that the aim of the activity is to build sentences which describe Mark's family tree using the word cards.

2. To show students what they are supposed to do, tell them that Mark introduces himself in the first sentence and starts with the word card *Hello*. Write this on the board/OHP, then ask students to look at the word cards and to call out which words they think Mark uses to introduce himself. When they have worked it out, write the complete sentence on the board/OHP (= *My name is Mark.*)

3. Tell students that they should work their way *down* the family tree starting with Peter. Draw their attention to the punctuation on some of the cards (commas, full stops, dashes, capital letters) and advise them to use this to help them make the right sentences. Use the first sentence on the board/OHP as an example, where Mark is followed by a full stop.

4. Allow students about ten to fifteen minutes to form sentences using the word cards. While they are working, walk around and help out where necessary.

5. When all pairs/small groups have finished, go through the complete text together by asking individual students to read out each full sentence.

6. **Note:** Different versions of the order of the text are possible, as long as the sentences are correct according to the family tree illustration.

Extension activity
You could ask students to draw a simplified version of their own family tree and write a short text about it similar to the text in the activity.
This could then form part of their personal *Language Portfolio*.

NEXT STARTER Unit 2

Activity 4   Family matters

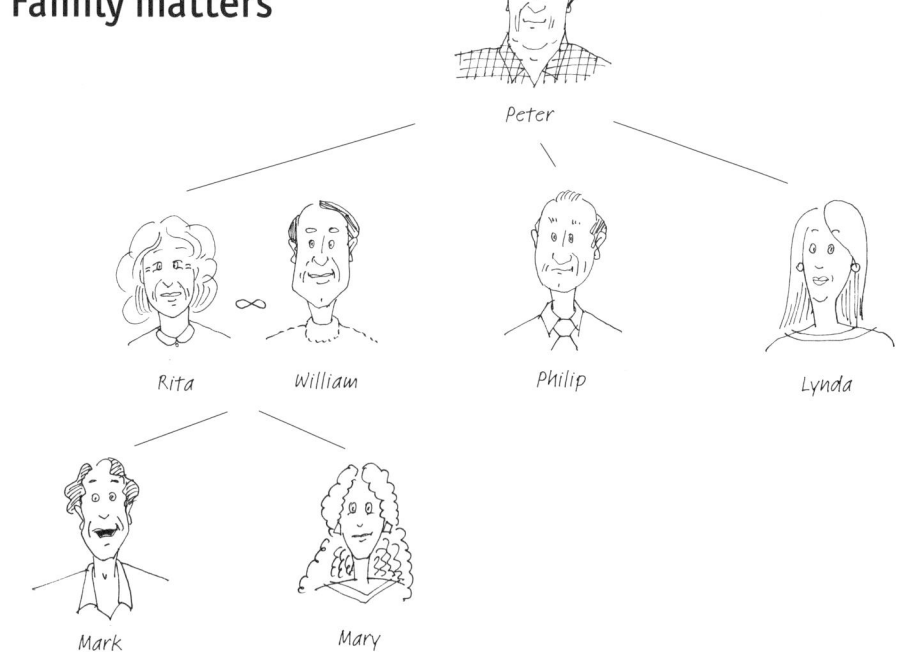

Hello,	my	name	is	Mark.
My	grandfather	is	Peter.	My
grandfather	has	three	children –	Rita,
Philip	and	Lynda.	My	mother
is	Rita	and	my	father
is	William.	I	have	a
sister.	Her	name	is	Mary.

NEXT STARTER — Unit 3

Activity 5   Is it true?

Teacher's notes

Activity
pairs & whole class, interview, speaking

Aim
to win a competition by making correct guesses about a person

Focus
3rd person singular "s"
present simple questions with *do*
free time activities
agreeing, disagreeing

Can do
I can ask simple personal questions.

20–25 minutes

Preparation

Make one copy of the activity sheet for every two students in your class.

Procedure

The aim of this activity is for students to try to make correct guesses about what their teacher likes to do in his/her free time. As well as focusing on free time vocabulary, the activity encourages a friendly atmosphere between teacher and students without becoming too personal.

1. Put students in pairs and give each pair an activity sheet.

2. Explain that the task is to try to make correct guesses about you, the teacher.

3. Pairs should speculate about the truth of each statement. If they agree, they should tick the "true" column and if not, the "false" one. You might want to write a few simple phrases (*I think so. I think so too. I don't think so.*) on the board/OHP for agreeing and disagreeing.

4. When everyone is finished, students must check their answers by taking turns to interview the teacher. Each statement must be turned into a direct question with *Do you …?* Students get one point for every correct guess.

5. Students count their scores and the pair or pairs with the most correct answers are the winners.

Extension activity

Students could write a short text about their teacher to put in their personal *Language Portfolio*.

NEXT STARTER   Unit 3

Activity 5   Is it true?

	True	False
1. Our teacher reads English books and newspapers.		
2. Our teacher plays tennis.		
3. Our teacher listens to pop music.		
4. Our teacher likes sports on TV.		
5. Our teacher plays the guitar.		
6. Our teacher surfs the Internet.		
7. Our teacher meets friends at a pub.		
8. Our teacher plays with his or her children.		
9. Our teacher cooks.		
10. Our teacher speaks English with friends.		

NEXT STARTER   Unit 3

Activity 6   Work hard, play harder

Teacher's notes

Activity
whole class, interview, speaking

Aim
to interview other students to find out what free time activities they do

15–20 minutes

Focus
present simple questions with *Do you …?*
short answers *Yes, I do. / No, I don't.*
free time activities

Can do
I can say what I do in my free time.

Preparation

Cut out enough cards for the number of students in your class and distribute one to each of them.
If you have more than 18 students in your class, use duplicate cards.

Procedure

The aim of the activity is for students to ask each other what different free time activities they do to find out which student in the class is most active.

1. Tell students that they are going to walk around the class, asking each other a question based on the activity on their card using *Do you …?*, e.g. *In your free time, do you play tennis?* They should answer using the short forms *Yes, I do. / No, I don't.*

2. If the student they ask answers *No, I don't,* they should move on to another student and ask the question again until they receive a positive answer.

3. When students find someone who gives the answer *Yes, I do,* they should write the student's name on one of the lines provided on the card and then swap cards with that student. Students should look at the names already on their card and as far as possible ask other students whose names don't appear.

4. Students continue milling, asking their new question until they find someone who does the activity on the card, and the procedure is repeated.

5. Allow students about 10 minutes to do the activity. While they are doing this, write the names of all the students in the class on the board/OHP.

6. Stop the activity and ask students to sit down. Go through each name on the board/OHP, asking students to raise their hands if the student appears on the card they have. Count the number of hands and write the number next to the student's name. The student whose name appears on the largest number of cards is the most active and "wins".

NEXT STARTER   Unit 3

Activity 6   Work hard, play harder

In your free time …	play tennis	In your free time …	sing karaoke
In your free time …	read books	In your free time …	meet friends
In your free time …	listen to jazz	In your free time …	go to bars
In your free time …	play computer games	In your free time …	play chess
In your free time …	watch TV	In your free time …	play guitar
In your free time …	play football	In your free time …	read magazines
In your free time …	read newspapers	In your free time …	listen to the radio
In your free time …	dance salsa	In your free time …	go to restaurants
In your free time …	go to the disco	In your free time …	stay at home

NEXT STARTER   Unit 4

Activity 7   My dream workplace

Teacher's notes

Activity
pairwork, partner dictation, speaking

Aim
to dictate and draw the position of objects in a room

15–20 minutes

Focus
prepositions of place *(next to, in, on, under)*
there is/there are
objects and furniture in a workplace

Can do
I can describe my ideal workplace.
I can say where things are in a room.

Preparation

Copy one activity sheet per student.

Procedure

The object of the activity is to dictate a picture which a partner must reproduce as accurately as possible.

1. Distribute one copy of the worksheet to each student in the class.

2. If you're doing this activity as revision, brainstorm workplace furniture and objects vocabulary in a mindmap on the board/OHP. If you're not using the NEXT Starter coursebook, use whatever vocabulary and prepositions you have in your coursebook.

3. Ask students first to draw the objects which they would like in their dream workplace in different places in the upper room picture on the worksheet. They should do this alone and not show anyone. With a more able class, allow them to be creative and add other objects and furniture which they may know in English (e.g. sofa, coffee machine, etc.). Advise students to limit themselves to positioning objects and furniture that they can describe using *next to, in, on* and *under*.

4. Get students into pairs. Student "A" describes where each of his/her objects is, e.g. *The CD player is on the bookshelf* or *There's a CD player on the bookshelf*. His/her partner should listen and draw the items in the correct place on the lower room picture on their activity sheet. This procedure is then repeated by Student "B".

5. After pairs have finished describing and drawing, they should compare what they've drawn to check that they have understood correctly. If there are differences, students should tell their partners the correct position, e.g. *The computer is on the table,* etc.

Extension activity
Students could write a short description of their dream workplace to accompany the picture that they have drawn. The picture and their description could then form part of their personal **Language Portfolio**.

NEXT STARTER Unit 4

Activity 7 My dream workplace

My dream workplace

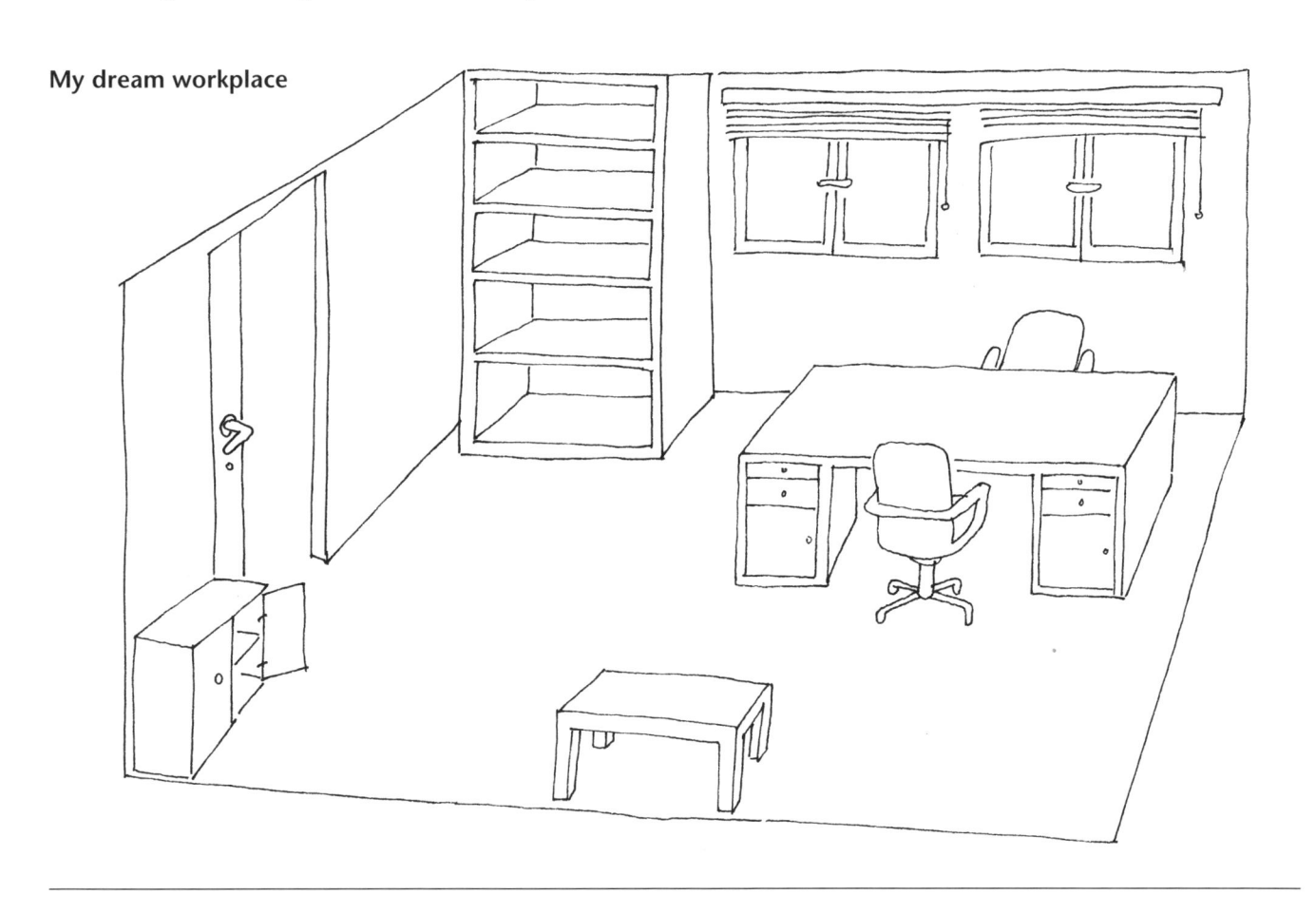

My partner's dream workplace

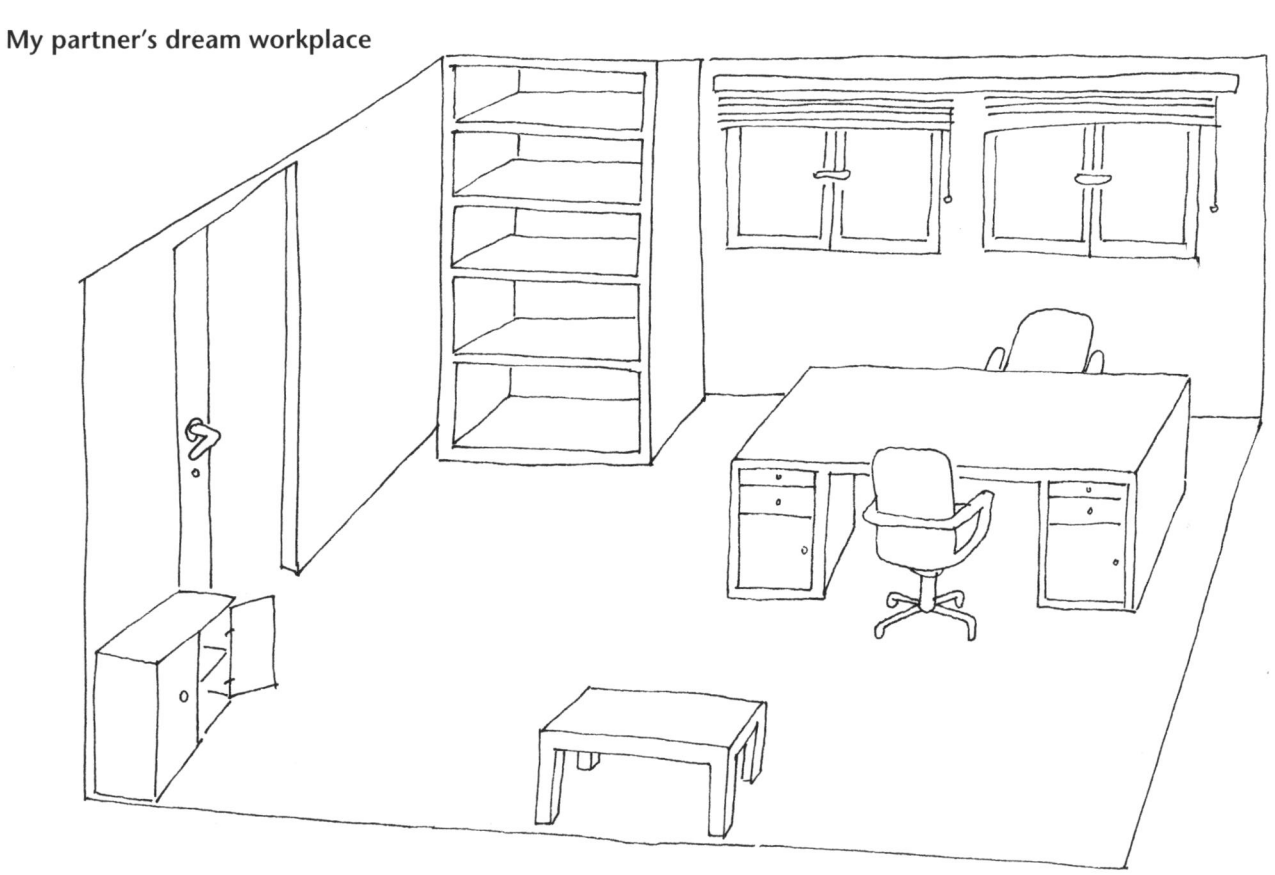

© 2007 Hueber Verlag · This sheet may be photocopied and used in class.

NEXT STARTER   Unit 4

Activity 8   Who in the world?

Teacher's notes

Activity
whole class, interview, speaking

Aim
to interview classmates and report findings

20 minutes

Focus
3rd person singular "s"
present simple questions with *do*
workplace, lifestyle

Can do
I can understand simple questions asking for personal information.
I can ask and answer simple personal questions.

Preparation

Copy one activity sheet for every student in the class or, if you want to make the activity shorter, copy one sheet for every two students and cut the sheet in half along the vertical middle line.

Procedure

The aim of the activity is for students to find out more about each other by asking questions and noting down the names of students who answer with *yes*.

1. Explain to students that they are going to ask each other questions and review the present simple question form *Do you …?*

2. Hand out the activity sheets to your students. If you have cut the sheet in two, give the half with the "has" statements to your less able students so they can always use the same question form *Do you have …?* (or *Have you got …?* if they have learned this form). Ask students to notice the question word *who* at the top of each statement box and remind them of its meaning.

3. Explain that the aim of the activity is to find out **who in the class does or has what.** Students will need to use the question form *Do you …?* to get the information necessary to complete the sentences on their cards.

4. Students should move about the classroom asking each partner one or two questions before moving on to a new partner. If their partner answers a question with *yes,* they should fill in the student's name. They are finished when they have completed every sentence with a name or when you feel the activity has gone on long enough.

5. Ask for feedback about the students in your class, for example *What can you tell me about Monika?* or *Does Niklas have a mobile phone with a camera?*

NEXT STARTER Unit 4

Activity 8   Who in the world?

Who? Name: _____ works in an office.	**Who?** Name: _____ has a mobile phone with a camera.
Who? Name: _____ works at home.	**Who?** Name: _____ has a big family.
Who? Name: _____ writes emails.	**Who?** Name: _____ has a lot of free time.
Who? Name: _____ speaks two languages.	**Who?** Name: _____ has a visiting card.
Who? Name: _____ plays chess in his or her free time.	**Who?** Name: _____ has an interesting job.

© 2007 Hueber Verlag · This sheet may be photocopied and used in class.

NEXT STARTER   Unit 5

Activity 9   Numbermania!

Teacher's notes	**Activity** pairwork, quiz, speaking	**Focus** numbers 21–100
15–20 minutes	**Aim** to win points by answering quiz questions correctly	**Can do** *I can say and understand numbers from 21 to 100.*

Preparation

Make one copy of the activity sheet for every two students in your class. Cut the sheets in half along the dotted line.

Procedure

The object of the activity is to win points by answering the questions correctly.

1. Get students into pairs and give one student the Partner A questionnaire and the other the Partner B questionnaire. Tell students not to show each other their questions.

2. Students take turns reading out their questions to each other. It is important that students concentrate on saying the numbers correctly when reading out the questions. You should walk around the classroom, listening in and helping when a student is uncertain.

3. Their partner should say which answer he/she thinks is correct. If he/she is right, the student who asked the question should make a tick beside the question.

4. When students have finished, they should count their partner's total points to see which of them was the winner. If there is a tie (i.e. they both have the same number of points), they should think of 5 numbers each between 21 and 100 and dictate them to their partner. The person with the best dictation results is then the winner. If the result of the number dictation doesn't break the tie, then they are both winners.

NEXT STARTER   Unit 5

Activity 9   Numbermania!

Partner A

Quiz questions for partner B	Answers
Are there 26 or 28 letters in the alphabet?	There are 26.
Are there 48 or 50 stars on the American flag?	There are 50.
Are there 30 or 31 days in September?	There are 30.
Are there 25 or 27 countries in the EU?	There are 27.
Are there 80 or 100 calories in a small banana?	There are 100.
Are there 24 or 32 figures in a chess game?	There are 32.

Partner B

Quiz questions for partner A	Answers
Are there 52 or 53 weeks in a year?	There are 52.
Are there 30 or 31 days in July?	There are 31.
Are there 60 or 75 calories in a small apple?	There are 75.
Are there 45 or 48 countries in Europe?	There are 48.
Are there 32 or 36 cards in a game of Skat?	There are 32.
Are there 51 or 61 airports in Germany?	There are 61.

© 2007 Hueber Verlag · This sheet may be photocopied and used in class.

NEXT STARTER   Unit 5

Activity 10   This is my life

Teacher's notes

Activity
whole class, information exchange, speaking

Aim
to complete a life line with details from a fictitious life

20 minutes

Focus
past simple
a life history

Can do
I can understand a short text that describes someone's life history in simple sentences.

Preparation

Make one copy of Sheet A for every 4 students in the class. Cut out each life line on Sheet A along the cutting lines so that you have one life line for every student.

Make one copy of Sheet B for every 12 students in your class and cut out the 12 texts. If you have more than 12 students, simply use duplicate texts.

Procedure

The aim of the activity is to complete Peter's life line by gathering information.

1. Review the past simple if necessary.

2. Hand out the life lines and explain to students that they are going to find out about some events in the life of a man called Peter. They should complete the life line with short notes as in the example *was born* on their life line sheet. **Point out that knowing Peter's date of birth will enable them to work out other dates in his life.**

3. Hand out the 12 texts describing an event in Peter's life, one to each student. Ask students not to show each other their texts.

4. Students should make a note about the event on their life line. With an able class, you could ask students to study their piece of information for a few minutes so that they can tell the others about it during the activity rather than reading every word out from the piece of paper.

5. Students should then walk around the classroom asking each other *What can you tell me about Peter?* (You can write this on the board/OHP if you like).

6. Each time they get a new piece of information, they should make a note on their life line. When their life line is complete, they can sit down.

7. Ask individual students to tell you what happened on the dates in the life line. Students should try to make complete sentences about Peter's life.

Extension activity

With an able class, students could write Peter's life story in sentences from their life line notes. This text could then form a part of their personal *Language Portfolio*.

Key
Life line: Peter Smith
1930: was born
1936: started school
1948: finished school
1949: started a job (bank)
1958: met Molly
1960: married Molly
1962: Steven born
1965: opened bookshop
1985: travelled to Paris
1990: son/shop assistant in bookshop
1995: grandson born
2000: finished work
Today: old but happy

NEXT STARTER   Unit 5

Activity 10   This is my life   Sheet A

Life line:	Peter Smith					
	1930: was born	1936: ___	1948: ___	1949: ___	1958: ___	1960: ___
1962: ___	1965: ___	1985: ___	1990: ___	1995: ___	2000: ___	today: ___

Life line:	Peter Smith					
	1930: was born	1936: ___	1948: ___	1949: ___	1958: ___	1960: ___
1962: ___	1965: ___	1985: ___	1990: ___	1995: ___	2000: ___	today: ___

Life line:	Peter Smith					
	1930: was born	1936: ___	1948: ___	1949: ___	1958: ___	1960: ___
1962: ___	1965: ___	1985: ___	1990: ___	1995: ___	2000: ___	today: ___

Life line:	Peter Smith					
	1930: was born	1936: ___	1948: ___	1949: ___	1958: ___	1960: ___
1962: ___	1965: ___	1985: ___	1990: ___	1995: ___	2000: ___	today: ___

© 2007 Hueber Verlag · This sheet may be photocopied and used in class.

NEXT STARTER Unit 5

Activity 10   This is my life   Sheet B

Peter started school when he was six.	Peter finished school when he was 18.
Peter started a job at a bank in 1949.	When he was 28, Peter met a young woman named Molly.
Peter married Molly in 1960.	Peter and Molly were happy. Their son, Steven, was born in 1962.
When he was 35, Peter opened a small bookshop.	In 1985 Peter travelled to Paris with Molly for a holiday.
In 1990 his son started work as a shop assistant in Peter's bookshop.	When Peter was 65, his grandson was born.
Peter finished work when he was 70.	Today Peter and Molly are old but they are happy.

NEXT STARTER — Unit 6

Activity 11 A holiday romance

Teacher's notes

Activity
pairwork, jigsaw text, reading

Aim
to put a text together by matching pictures and sentences
to put verbs into the correct verb form

Focus
past simple verb forms (regular and irregular)

Can do
I can understand a simple conversation or text about someone's holiday.

20–25 minutes

Preparation

Copy one sheet for every two students in the class. Cut the activity in half along the dotted line between the pictures and the text. Cut the text into strips along the cutting lines so that there are 12 text strips for every two students and keep each set of 12 strips together with a paper clip.

Procedure

The aim of the activity is to use the pictures as an aid to putting the text in the right order.
Students should look for the strip of text that matches each separate picture.

1. Tell your class that they are going to read a story about a man's holiday. Explain that stories are usually told in the past simple tense. With your class brainstorm all the past tense verbs they have learned that they can think of and write these on the board or on an overhead transparency in two columns, one for regular and one for irregular verbs. Ask for the matching infinitive forms.

2. Give pairs the picture story (the top half of the activity sheet) first and say that these are the pictures that go with the text. Ask them to look at the pictures together and help each other to work out what the story is about. (Allow them to talk to each other in German at this point, if they prefer.) Meanwhile, erase the verbs from the board or switch off the overhead.

3. Now give pairs the 12 text strips and ask them to match one text strip with each picture so that the text is in the right order. Move around helping and explaining any unfamiliar words if necessary.

4. Finally, pairs should fill in the appropriate regular or irregular past tense form of the missing verbs in the sentences.

5. Check the story and the past tense verb forms with the class by getting them to read out their texts. Make sure that they have all understood the gist of the story.

6. Only the last two sentences are in the present tense. Ask the class why they think this is so. (= They describe the present, not past or finished events.)

NEXT STARTER   Unit 6

Activity 11   A holiday romance

John _flew_	(fly) to Italy for a holiday.
He _____	(stay) at a 3-star hotel.
Every day he _____	(go) to a sandy beach and relaxed in the sun.
Every evening he _____	(have) dinner at an excellent restaurant by the sea.
One evening, Maria _____	(be) his waitress. She was very attractive.
When she _____	(give) him a glass of red wine, he dropped the glass.
Maria _____	(have) red wine all over her clothes.
John _____	(be) sad. Next day he asked Maria to have a cup of coffee with him.
Soon they _____	(be) in love.
They _____	(marry) in Italy.
Now they live in England and have three children.	
And every summer they go to Italy on holiday!	

NEXT STARTER Unit 6

Activity 12   Where's the word?

Teacher's notes	Activity pairwork, game, vocabulary	Focus *Is there …?* numbers
15–20 minutes	Aim to identify words in a grid by finding out what letters are in the spaces	the alphabet unit vocabulary

Preparation

Make one copy of the activity sheet for each pair of students. Cut along the dotted line.

Procedure

This activity is based on the game "Battleships" (German: "Schiffe versenken") but in this version students must identify the words hidden in the grids, not ships.

1. Give one half of the worksheet to Partner A and the other to Partner B. Tell students not to show their half to their partner.

2. Ask students if they know the game "Battleships". If they do, tell them that this activity is based on the same rules, but with words instead of ships.

3. Explain the rules to any students who are not familiar with the game. Students have to ask each other questions as in the example given, e.g. *Is there a letter in A3?*, to try to find letters in their blank grid which make up words their partner has in his/her completed grid. Their partner answers either *Yes, it's (B).* or *No, there isn't.* Draw students' attention to the list under their blank grid (under **You need:**) to find out what kinds of words they are looking for. Once students have enough letters to guess the word, they can ask their partner *Is the word from A3 to A7 _____?* Write this question on the board/OHP.

4. Students should take turns asking and answering until they have both found all of their partner's words and written the letters in the correct boxes on their blank grid.

Extension activity (or for pairs who finish more quickly) Get students to choose three of the words they have found and to write three sentences using them. They then exchange sentences with their partner, who checks that what they have written is correct.

NEXT STARTER   Unit 6

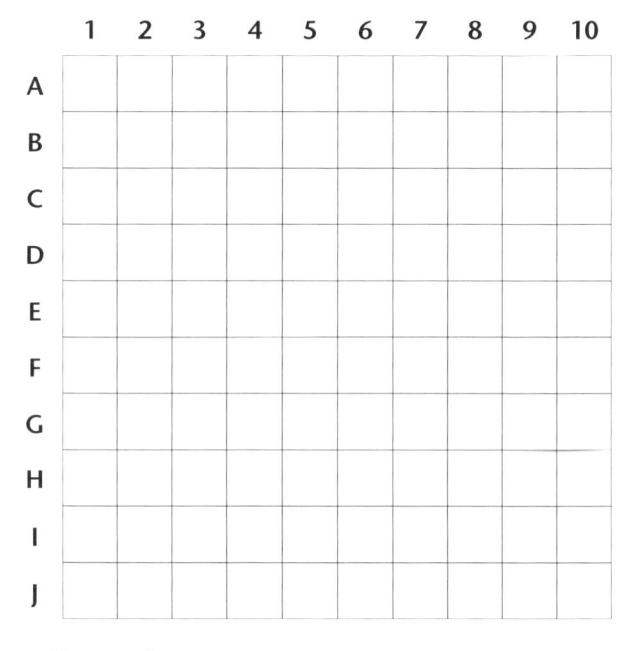

Activity 12   Where's the word?

Find the words in your partner's grid.

e.g. → *Is there a letter in A3?*
      → *Yes, it's (B).* or *No, there isn't.*

Partner A

	1	2	3	4	5	6	7	8	9	10
A	W			S		A	W	F	U	L
B	E			L						
C	D			E						
D	N			P						
E	E			T		G	R	E	A	T
F	S									
G	D		T	H	U	R	S	D	A	Y
H	A									
I	Y		D	R	O	V	E			
J										

	1	2	3	4	5	6	7	8	9	10
A										
B										
C										
D										
E										
F										
G										
H										
I										
J										

Your words:
– Two days of the week: WEDNESDAY; THURSDAY
– Two adjectives: AWFUL; GREAT
– Two past tense verbs: SLEPT; DROVE

You need:
– Two past tense verbs
– Two kinds of holiday
– Two plural words

Find the words in your partner's grid.

e.g. → *Is there a letter in A3?*
      → *Yes, it's (B).* or *No, there isn't.*

Partner B

	1	2	3	4	5	6	7	8	9	10
A			A		W	E	N	T		R
B			D							E
C			V				P			L
D	D		E				E			A
E	R		N				O			X
F	A		T				P			I
G	N		U				L			N
H	K		R				E			G
I			E							
J		C	O	U	N	T	R	I	E	S

	1	2	3	4	5	6	7	8	9	10
A										
B										
C										
D										
E										
F										
G										
H										
I										
J										

Your words:
– Two past tense verbs: WENT; DRANK
– Two kinds of holiday: ADVENTURE; RELAXING
– Two plural words: PEOPLE; COUNTRIES

You need:
– Two days of the week
– Two adjectives
– Two past tense verbs

© 2007 Hueber Verlag · This sheet may be photocopied and used in class.

NEXT A1 Unit 1

Activity 13   Find your partner

Teacher's notes	**Activity** whole class, role play, speaking	**Focus** present tense; verb *to be* names and nationalities meeting/greeting/introducing
15–20 minutes	**Aim** to find a specific partner by introducing yourself	**Can do** I can introduce myself and others. I can say where I'm from.

Preparation

Make one copy of the sheet and cut it into 20 strips.
Be sure to keep **corresponding** pairs of strips together.

Procedure

The aim of this activity is to use the target language, saying your name and where you're from, to find a specific partner in the classroom.

1. Count out the role cards you need for the activity. If you have an odd number of students, join in. If you have fewer than 20 students, use fewer role cards, but be sure that you have included corresponding role cards.

2. Shuffle the strips and hand them out, one to each student. Ask them not to show their role card to anyone.

3. Explain that everyone in the class is taking on a fictitious identity. They are the person in the first line on their role card and they're looking for the person described in the second line. To find their partner, they will mix with their classmates, introduce themselves and say where they are from. **Note:** Both the name **and** nationality are important in finding the right partner, since several people have either similar names or the same nationality.

4. Demonstrate the language students will need to find their partner. Say *Hello. I'm Maria from Spain. And you? What's your name? Where are you from?* and get a response from one or two of your students. Then ask everyone to stand up and begin milling.

5. When partners have found each other, they can sit down together. When everyone is sitting, ask students to introduce their partners. *This is Franz from Austria. And this is Jana from Poland.*

NEXT A1   Unit 1

Activity 13   Find your partner

You: Maria from Italy. **Your partner:** Peter from England.	**You:** Susanne from Germany. **Your partner:** Patrick from Ireland.
You: Peter from England. **Your partner:** Maria from Italy.	**You:** Patrick from Ireland. **Your partner:** Susanne from Germany.
You: Maria from Spain. **Your partner:** Martin from Germany.	**You:** Paul from England. **Your partner:** Martina from Austria.
You: Martin from Germany. **Your partner:** Maria from Spain.	**You:** Martina from Austria. **Your partner:** Paul from England.
You: Kathy from Canada. **Your partner:** Peter from Switzerland.	**You:** Franz from Austria. **Your partner:** Jana from Poland.
You: Peter from Switzerland. **Your partner:** Kathy from Canada.	**You:** Jana from Poland. **Your partner:** Franz from Austria.
You: John from Canada. **Your partner:** Mitsuko from Japan.	**You:** Robert from Scotland. **Your partner:** Susan from Australia.
You: Mitsuko from Japan. **Your partner:** John from Canada.	**You:** Susan from Australia. **Your partner:** Robert from Scotland.
You: Marco from Italy. **Your partner:** Myriam from Malta.	**You:** Mike from Australia. **Your partner:** Olivia from Ireland.
You: Myriam from Malta. **Your partner:** Marco from Italy.	**You:** Olivia from Ireland. **Your partner:** Mike from Australia.

© 2007 Hueber Verlag · This sheet may be photocopied and used in class.

NEXT A1   Unit 1

Activity 14   Classroom English

Teacher's notes	Activity pairwork or group work, matching, reading	Focus classroom English (instructions) the imperative
15–20 minutes	Aim to match sentence beginnings and endings to form instructions which are commonly found in coursebooks	

Preparation

Copy one activity sheet for every pair or group of 2 to 4 students. Cut out the cards, mix and keep each set of 20 cards separate.

Procedure

The aim of this activity is to give students practice in learning the language of typical coursebook and classroom instructions.

1. Ask your students to spend a moment leafing through their coursebooks and noticing some of the language used at the start of activities to instruct students what to do. Elicit some examples from your students and write a few of them on the board/OHP.

2. Explain to students that they are going to practise forming similar instructions to help them learn these typical and necessary expressions.

3. Get students into pairs or groups of up to 4. Give each pair or group a set of the 20 cards and explain that 10 of the cards are sentence beginnings and 10 are sentence endings. The punctuation will give students information as to which part of the sentence they have in front of them; i.e. capital letters for sentence beginnings and full stops for sentence endings.

4. Ask students to form 10 sentences that are typical "classroom English" instructions. Although there is sometimes more than one possible way to combine the words, they should look for the way that enables them to use up all the cards. While they are working, walk around the classroom, observing and helping if necessary.

5. When everyone is finished, check the answers together as a class. If students have come up with different combinations than the solution suggested here, acknowledge the sentences if they are possible and discuss why not if they are not. You could then ask students to suggest other possible sentence endings for the 10 beginnings.

Key
Listen to / the CD.
Read / the dialogue.
Write / a sentence.
Tick / the right answer.
Match / the words to make pairs.
Work / in groups.
Complete / the table.
Look at / the picture.
Put the words / in the correct order.
Say / goodbye to the others.

NEXT A1 Unit 1

Activity 14   Classroom English

Listen to …	… the CD.
Read …	… the dialogue.
Write …	… a sentence.
Tick …	… the right answer.
Match …	… the words to make pairs.
Work …	… in groups.
Complete …	… the table.
Look at …	… the picture.
Put the words …	… in the correct order.
Say …	… goodbye to the others.

NEXT A1 Unit 2

Activity 15   Can you?

Teacher's notes	Activity whole class, class survey, speaking	Focus *can/can't* skills
20 minutes	Aim to gather information about what students in the class can do	

Preparation

Copy the activity sheet once for every 12 students in the class. Cut out the 12 *Most of us can …* cards and keep the sets in separate bags or envelopes. If you have more than 12 students, use duplicate cards.

Procedure

The aim of this activity is for students to carry out a survey of what skills they and the other members of the class have by asking questions.

1. Give each student a card with a *Most of us can …* statement. Explain that they are going to do a class survey to find out what skills students in the class have by asking each other questions. First elicit the correct question form for them to do this (= *Can you* plus verb) and put an example on the board/OHP; e.g. *Can you ski?* Some of the *Most of us can …* statements contain the pronoun *our* which must also be changed when asking a direct question. Demonstrate this on the board/OHP. Write *Most of us can say our telephone number in English,* underline the word *our*, and get students to formulate the question *Can you say your telephone number …?* Leave both example sentences on the board/OHP.

2. Ask students to read the statement on their card, and if they can do the activity, they should make a mark (e.g. a tick or short vertical line) or write their name on the back of the card. If they are not able to do the activity, they shouldn't write anything.

3. Get students to move around the classroom and interview one partner at a time. Each time they get a positive answer (i.e. *Yes, I can.*), they should make a mark on their card or write the student's name.

4. When everyone has had time to interview all the other students, or when you feel the activity has gone on long enough, ask students to sit down.

5. Get students to report back to the class about their findings in complete sentences, e.g. *Two students can speak French.* or *Maria and Hannes can speak French.* Write the results in numbers for each of the 12 statements on the board/OHP so that everyone can see which skill or skills are shared by the most students.

NEXT A1 Unit 2

Activity 15 Can you?

Most of us can send an email.	Most of us can play golf.
Most of us can ski.	Most of us can cook.
Most of us can drive a car.	Most of us can play an instrument.
Most of us can say our nationality in English.	Most of us can say "verheiratet" in English.
Most of us can say our phone number in English.	Most of us can spell our first name in English.
Most of us can speak French.	Most of us can sing.

NEXT A1 Unit 2

Activity 16   Alphabingo

Teacher's notes	**Activity** whole class, game	**Focus** letters of the alphabet
15 – 20 minutes	**Aims** to win a game by understanding and saying letters of the alphabet	**Can do** *I can spell words.*

Preparation

Copy and cut out enough bingo cards for the number of students in your class and distribute them. If you have more than 12 students, you can give the same card to more than one student.

Procedure

This activity is the game "Bingo!" played with letters instead of numbers. The game is made more challenging by not having the letters on the cards in alphabetical order. The object of the game is to get a bingo.

1. Explain to students that the aim of the game is to cross out all of the letters on their card to win, at which point they should shout out *Bingo!*

2. Tell them that you are going to call out letters of the alphabet **at random**. Students should listen and if they have the letter that you call out on their bingo card, they should cross it out. **Note:** To keep track of which letters you have already called out, mark the letters off on the letter checklist provided below.

3. The game continues until one student has crossed out all of his/her letters and calls out *Bingo!*

4. Ask the winning student to read back the letters on his/her card to check that they crossed out the correct letters.

Teacher's letter checklist:

A	B	C	D	E	F	G	H	I	J	K	L	M	N	O	P	Q	R	S	T	U	V	W	X	Y	Z

NEXT A1   Unit 2

Activity 16   Alphabingo

I	A	S
K	W	M
Y	U	G

L	H	Z
J	B	V
X	T	N

Y	U	A
I	K	O
M	C	W

B	X	D
J	P	V
N	Z	L

K	C	A
M	E	O
Y	W	Q

X	Z	F
N	D	L
P	B	R

Y	S	O
E	C	Q
G	M	A

D	B	F
N	H	Z
P	R	T

S	U	A
O	E	G
C	I	Q

H	J	T
F	R	D
P	V	B

S	G	Q
K	E	W
C	U	I

H	J	F
V	R	L
T	X	D

© 2007 Hueber Verlag · This sheet may be photocopied and used in class.

NEXT A1 Unit 3

Activity 17 What's the word?

Teacher's notes	Activity	Focus
	pairs, acrostic puzzle, vocabulary definitions	food and drink, colours, days of the week, adverbs of frequency
15–20 minutes	**Aims** to solve a word puzzle with unit vocabulary	

Preparation

Copy one activity sheet per student and distribute.

Procedure

The aim of this activity is to solve a word puzzle by filling in items of vocabulary and grammar which students have encountered in the unit.

1. Students can work alone or in pairs.

2. Tell students that they should read the clues at the bottom of the activity sheet to complete the missing words in the puzzle and find out the central vertical key word.

3. When they have filled in the words and know the central key word, they should answer the question under the puzzle. **The solution is "meat".**

Key
1. vegetables
2. ketchup
3. burger
4. lemon
5. tuna
6. Thursday
7. favourite
8. milk
9. breakfast
10. green

www.hueber.de/next   Web code for this Unit: XA1T03

NEXT A1   Unit 3

Activity 17   What's the word?

What kind of food does this person never eat? _____

Clues:

1. Potatoes, carrots and cabbages are all _____.
2. It's red and you sometimes eat it with chips.
3. It's meat and it's usually in a bread roll. It's popular at fast food restaurants.
4. It's a yellow fruit and you sometimes have a bit of it in mineral water.
5. It's a type of fish and you sometimes eat it in a salad.
6. The day after Wednesday.
7. Something you like best is your _____.
8. It's white and you can drink it in tea.
9. The meal you eat at the start of the day.
10. The colour of broccoli.

NEXT A1 Unit 3

Activity 18   Food and drink

Teacher's notes		
Activity whole class, milling activity, speaking		**Focus** the verb *to like* (question and short answer forms) 3rd person singular food and drink vocabulary
Aims to find out what students like to eat and drink by asking questions		
10–15 minutes		**Can do** I can ask what someone likes to eat and drink. I can say what I like to eat and drink.

Preparation

Copy one activity sheet per student and distribute.

Procedure

The aim of this activity is to find out what food and drink other students in the class like.

1. Elicit from students what question they have to ask to find out what food and drink other students like and don't like (= *Do you like …?*). Ask students what the two possible answers to this question are (= *Yes, I do. / No, I don't.*). For less able students, you could write the question and answers on the board/OHP.

2. Explain to students that they should walk around the classroom, asking and answering the questions. When they find someone who likes the food or drink item in the picture, they should write that student's name in the space provided in each box on the activity sheet.

Note: Emphasize that students should try to find a different person for each food or drink item as far as possible.
If you join in, you can help students with vocabulary or pronunciation tactfully.

3. At the end of the activity, ask a few individual students to tell the rest of the class what food and/or drink three people they found like (*Johann/Johanna likes …*).

NEXT A1 Unit 3

Activity 18   Food and drink

| Find someone who likes:

Name: _____ | Find someone who likes:

Name: _____ |
|---|---|
| Find someone who likes:

Name: _____ | Find someone who likes:

Name: _____ |
| Find someone who likes:

Name: _____ | Find someone who likes:

Name: _____ |
| Find someone who likes:

Name: _____ | Find someone who likes:

Name: _____ |
| Find someone who likes:

Name: _____ | Find someone who likes:

Name: _____ |

NEXT A1 Unit 4

Activity 19   Jenny's day

Teacher's notes	Activity whole class, information exchange, speaking	Focus daily routines telling the time
15–20 minutes	Aim to find out what someone does at a certain time of day	Can do I can say the time. I can describe some of the daily activities of others.

Preparation

Copy one picture sheet (Sheet A) for each student and one text box sheet (Sheet B) for every 12 students in the class. For this activity to work, you must use all 12 texts, so if you have fewer than 12 students, give your more able students two text cards each. If you have more than 12 students, simply duplicate a few texts. Cut out the 12 text boxes and keep each set of 12 in separate envelopes.

Procedure

The aim of the activity is to find out what Jenny does at 5 o'clock in the afternoon. There are 12 text cards giving information about Jenny's typical daily activities and when they take place, but 13 pictures on the picture sheets. To find the solution students must find out the 12 pieces of information on the text cards and match this information with the appropriate pictures on their picture sheets. **The picture left over at the end shows what Jenny does at 5 p.m.**

1. Hand out one picture sheet to each student. Explain that the pictures show activities that are part of a typical day for a young woman named Jenny.

2. Give each student at least one text card which describes one of Jenny's typical activities. Tell students to find the picture of their activity on their picture sheet and fill in the correct digital time (using **numbers,** not words) under the picture.

3. Get students to walk around, exchanging information about Jenny's day. To help them do this, write on the board/OHP: *What do you know about Jenny?* Each time they meet a new partner, they should ask this question. When they receive an answer, they should find the corresponding picture on their picture sheet and fill in the correct time below.

4. When students have filled in the times under 12 of the pictures, one picture will be left. Get them to answer the question at the bottom of their picture sheet. Ask a student to give you the answer.
(Solution: Jenny plays tennis at 5 in the afternoon.)

Extension activity
Ask students to put Jenny's activities in the correct order by numbering the pictures. Let them describe Jenny's day orally. To practise questions with *does,* let students ask and answer a question for each picture; e.g. *When does Jenny get up? She gets up at half past six/six thirty.* Finally, students could write a summary of Jenny's day by looking at their picture sheet with the digital times. Written texts can be included in students' personal *Language Portfolios.*

NEXT A1   Unit 4

Activity 19   Jenny's day   Sheet A

time: _____

time: _____

time: _____

time: _____

time: _____

time: _____

time: _____

time: _____

time: _____

time: _____

time: _____

time: _____

What does Jenny do at 5 o'clock in the afternoon?

NEXT A1 Unit 4

Activity 19   Jenny's day   Sheet B

Jenny gets up at half past six.	She finishes work at 3 o'clock.
She gives the cat its food at a quarter to seven in the morning.	She goes to the supermarket at a quarter past three.
She has breakfast at a quarter past seven.	She phones her mum at 4 in the afternoon.
She goes to work at 8 o'clock.	She meets a friend at a restaurant at half past six.
She has lunch with colleagues at 12 o'clock.	She watches TV at 9 o'clock in the evening.
She writes an email at 1 o'clock in the afternoon.	She goes to bed at 11 o'clock.

NEXT A1 Unit 4

Activity 20   Time Snap

Teacher's notes

Activity
group work, game, telling the time

Aim
to win a card game by matching analogue and digital times

Focus
analogue and digital times

Can do
I can say the time.

15–20 minutes

Preparation

Make one copy of the activity sheet for each group of 3 or 4 students. Cut out the cards with the analogue clock faces and the digital clocks and keep them separate.

Procedure

This activity is based on the game "Snap!" The aim of the game is to match the analogue clock face cards with their corresponding digital clock cards. The winner is the student with the most "tricks" (i.e. matched cards) at the end.

1. Get students into groups of three or four. Hand out the two separate piles of analogue clock faces and digital clocks to each group. Tell the groups to keep the piles separate and to shuffle them.

2. Tell students to place each shuffled pile face down on the desk.

3. Each student takes it in turn to take the top card from the digital clock pile first and place it down on the table so that everyone in the group can see it. They should then say the time aloud for the group, e.g. *It's twelve fifteen.*

4. The same student should then take the top card from the clock face pile and quickly place it on the desk next to the digital clock card. If the times are the same, anyone in the group can shout aloud *Snap!* The fastest student to shout *Snap!* must then say the correct analogue time, e.g. *It's quarter past twelve,* to win the trick, which they keep. If they say the time incorrectly, any other student in the group can say the correct time and they get to keep the trick.

5. Students continue until two matching cards appear again. If the cards do not match, then they are placed to one side in two separate piles and the game continues from point 3 above. When students reach the end of the piles of cards, they should reshuffle the two piles and carry on until all the cards have been matched or you think the game has gone on long enough.

NEXT A1   Unit 4

Activity 20   Time Snap

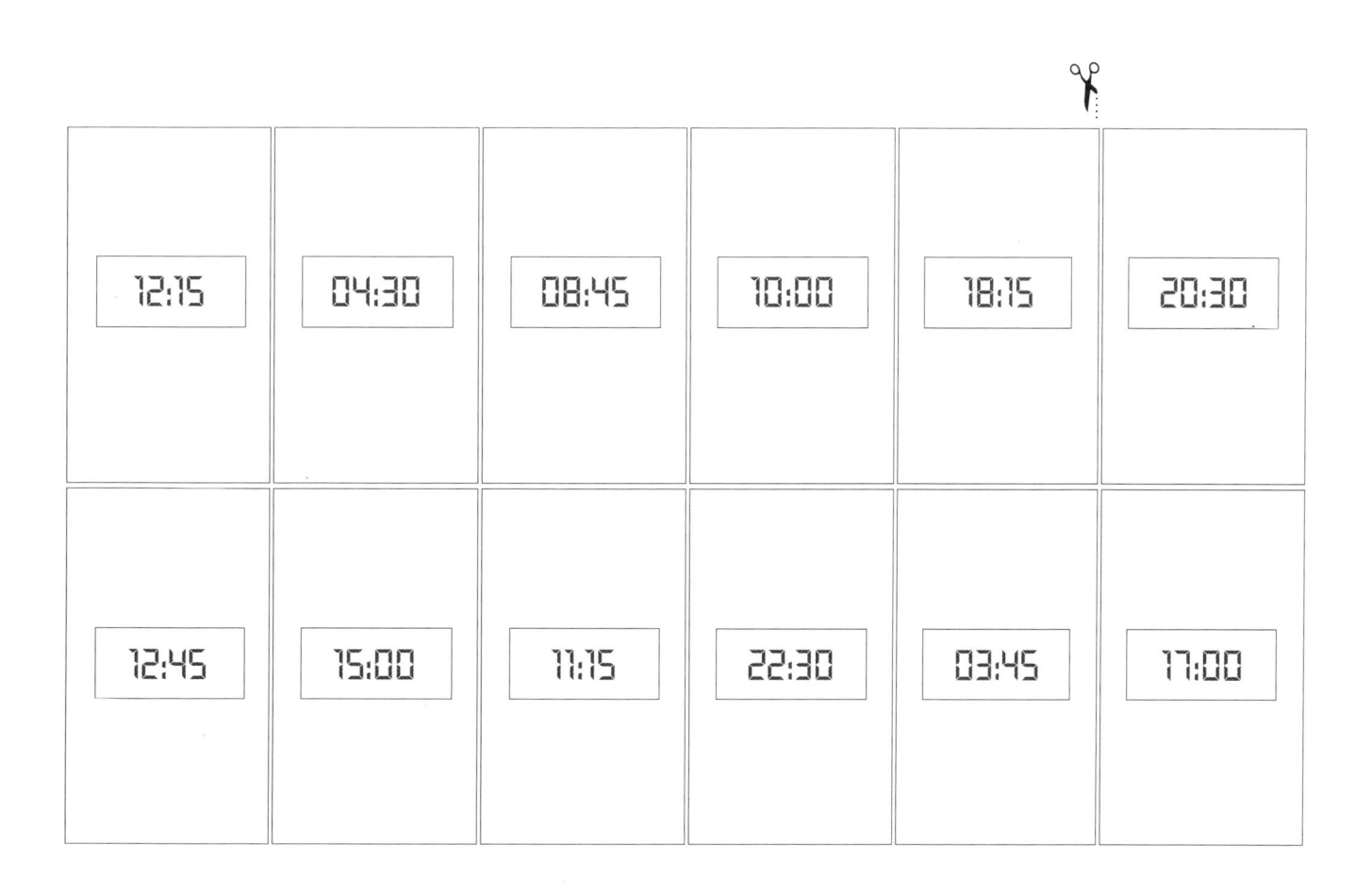

| 12:15 | 04:30 | 08:45 | 10:00 | 18:15 | 20:30 |

| 12:45 | 15:00 | 11:15 | 22:30 | 03:45 | 17:00 |

NEXT A1   Unit 5

Activity 21   History Quiz

Teacher's notes

Activity
whole class, quiz, speaking/listening

Aim
to guess the names of famous dead people

15–20 minutes

Focus
past simple tense
regular and irregular verbs
life stories

Can do
I can understand simple statements about another person's life history.

Preparation

For method **one**, make one copy of the quiz sheet. If you prefer a milling activity (method **two**), copy enough sheets so that everyone in the class can have one question and cut out the 14 quiz statements.

Procedure

The object of the activity is to guess who the famous dead people described here are.
Tell your class that they are going to play a quiz game. Review past tense verb forms if necessary.

Method one: a competition

1. Divide the class into two or more teams. Let each team choose a spokesman.

2. Begin with Team A. Read out question number one and let them confer. Then the spokesperson should give the answer. If it is correct, give the team a point. If the answer is incorrect, Team B can have a chance at the question. Teams may only give one answer, therefore they should confer and deliberate rather than spontaneously calling out their guesses!

3. Play until every team has had an equal number of chances to make a point. The team with the most points is the winner.

Method two: a milling activity with lots of opportunity for repetition

1. Give each student one of the 14 strips. It does not matter if there are duplicates. Let them read their text silently and identify the person described. If they don't know, they can come to you and you can whisper the famous person's name to them or write it down.

2. Then ask students to get up, and, meeting just one partner at a time, read out their quiz questions to each other. If they each can identify the other's historical person, then they may **trade** question strips and move on with a new question to a new partner.

3. They can keep meeting and trading until you think they've had time to hear most of the questions. Then ask them to sit down and let them read out the question they now have in their hands for the whole class to identify.

Key
1. Walt Disney
2. Cleopatra
3. John Lennon
4. Marlene Dietrich
5. Alfred Hitchcock
6. Princess Diana
7. Wolfgang Amadeus Mozart
8. Marie Tussaud
9. Shakespeare
10. Maria Callas
11. John F. Kennedy
12. Marilyn Monroe
13. Albert Einstein
14. Grace Kelly

NEXT A1   Unit 5

Activity 21   History Quiz

Who is this person?

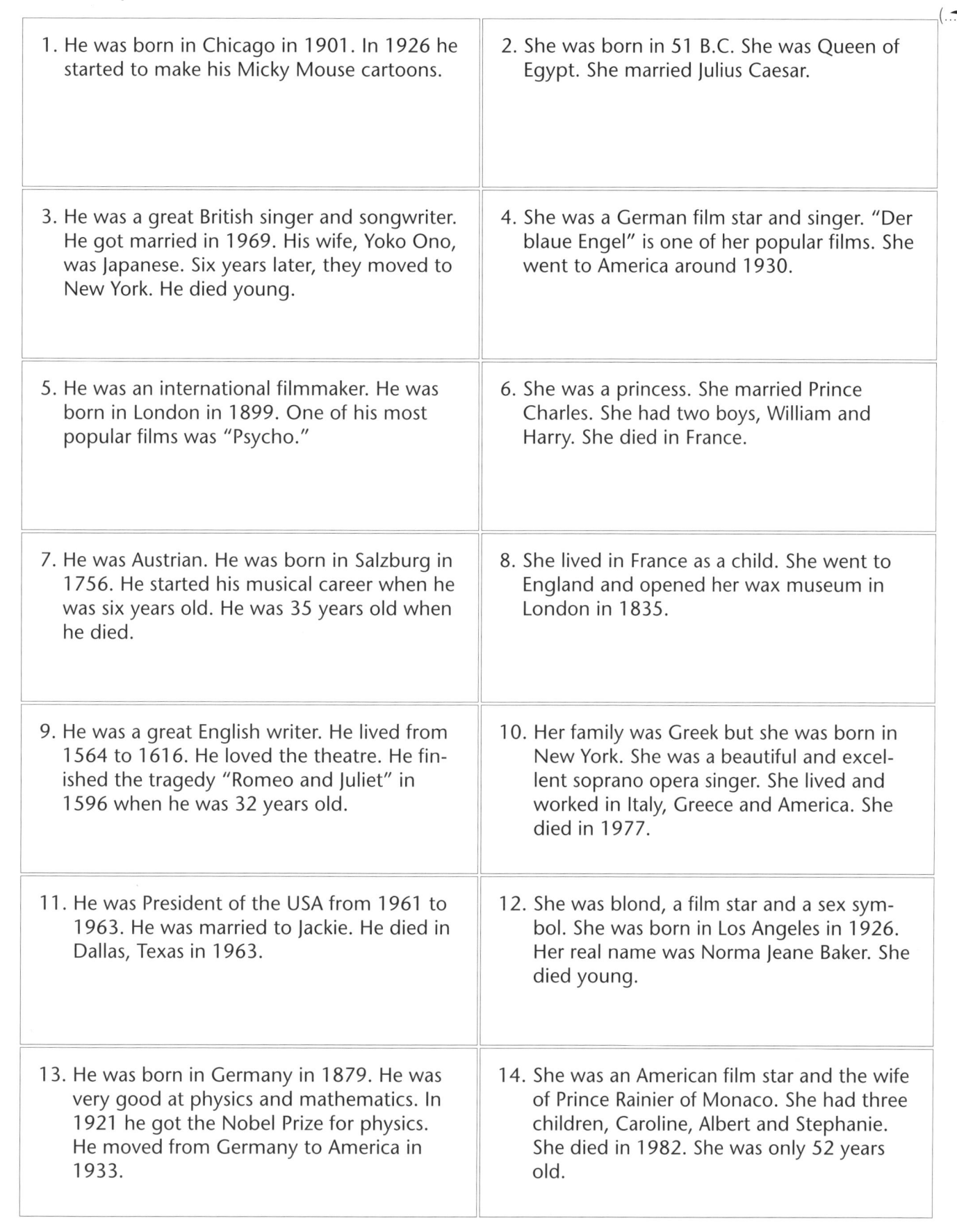

1. He was born in Chicago in 1901. In 1926 he started to make his Micky Mouse cartoons.	2. She was born in 51 B.C. She was Queen of Egypt. She married Julius Caesar.
3. He was a great British singer and songwriter. He got married in 1969. His wife, Yoko Ono, was Japanese. Six years later, they moved to New York. He died young.	4. She was a German film star and singer. "Der blaue Engel" is one of her popular films. She went to America around 1930.
5. He was an international filmmaker. He was born in London in 1899. One of his most popular films was "Psycho."	6. She was a princess. She married Prince Charles. She had two boys, William and Harry. She died in France.
7. He was Austrian. He was born in Salzburg in 1756. He started his musical career when he was six years old. He was 35 years old when he died.	8. She lived in France as a child. She went to England and opened her wax museum in London in 1835.
9. He was a great English writer. He lived from 1564 to 1616. He loved the theatre. He finished the tragedy "Romeo and Juliet" in 1596 when he was 32 years old.	10. Her family was Greek but she was born in New York. She was a beautiful and excellent soprano opera singer. She lived and worked in Italy, Greece and America. She died in 1977.
11. He was President of the USA from 1961 to 1963. He was married to Jackie. He died in Dallas, Texas in 1963.	12. She was blond, a film star and a sex symbol. She was born in Los Angeles in 1926. Her real name was Norma Jeane Baker. She died young.
13. He was born in Germany in 1879. He was very good at physics and mathematics. In 1921 he got the Nobel Prize for physics. He moved from Germany to America in 1933.	14. She was an American film star and the wife of Prince Rainier of Monaco. She had three children, Caroline, Albert and Stephanie. She died in 1982. She was only 52 years old.

NEXT A1   Unit 5

Activity 22   What was the weather like?

Teacher's notes

Activity
pairwork, information gap, speaking

Aim
to find out what the weather was like at a certain place and time

15–20 minutes

Focus
words to describe the weather
past simple questions with *was*

Can do
I can describe yesterday's and today's weather in simple words.

Preparation

Copy one activity sheet for every two students in the class. Cut the sheets in half along the dotted line.

Procedure

The aim of the activity is to find out what the weather was like at a certain time and place by asking questions about and describing the weather based on a map.

1. If necessary, review vocabulary for describing the weather and the symbols used on weather maps, as well as the questions which can be asked to find out about the weather, e.g. *What was the weather like in …/on …?*

2. Get students into pairs. Give each student a Partner A or Partner B questionnaire. Explain that they should find out what the weather was like in the places given. Elicit what question they should use to do this (= *What was the weather like in …?*). With a less able class, you may also want to write this on the board/OHP. Emphasize that they should use the temperatures to decide if it was *hot, warm, cool* or *cold*. Students take turns asking questions to find out about the weather on a certain day in a certain city in the British Isles or Germany. They should write down the answers in note form, i.e. *hot, warm, cool, cold, sunny, cloudy, rainy, snowy, windy*. Move around the room as they work and help or correct tactfully as necessary.

3. When students have finished, check the answers together as a class by asking the questions yourself.

4. End the activity by asking students what the weather was like today in their town/city/country.

NEXT A1 Unit 5

Activity 22   What was the weather like?

Partner A

Ask your partner about the weather in the British Isles on May 25th.	Answers for your partner's questions:
Where: Loch Ness **Answer:** _____ **Where:** Glasgow **Answer:** _____ **Where:** Belfast **Answer:** _____ **Where:** Norwich **Answer:** _____ **Where:** London **Answer:** _____	Kiel 7° Berlin 5° Frankfurt 2° Stuttgart -3° Munich -5°

Partner B

Ask your partner about the weather in Germany on December 19th.	Answers for your partner's questions:
Where: Kiel **Answer:** _____ **Where:** Berlin **Answer:** _____ **Where:** Frankfurt **Answer:** _____ **Where:** Stuttgart **Answer:** _____ **Where:** Munich **Answer:** _____	Loch Ness 14° Glasgow 14° Belfast 13° Norwich 18° London 20°

© 2007 Hueber Verlag · This sheet may be photocopied and used in class.

NEXT A1 Unit 6

Activity 23   What did you do in Paris?

Teacher's notes

Activity
whole class, information exchange, speaking

Aim
to "complete" a fictitious holiday by collecting the appropriate activity cards

20–25 minutes

Focus
past simple questions with *did*
holiday activities

Can do
I can talk about a past holiday.
I can name common holiday activities.

Preparation

Make one copy of Sheet A for every 4 students in your class. Cut all the A sheets into the 4 separate holiday cards. Copy Sheet B once for every 20 students in the class and cut out the 20 phrases. You must have one holiday card and one phrase slip for every student in the class.

Procedure

The aim of the activity is to collect all of the activity slips that go with "your" holiday.

1. If necessary, review the question form in the past simple: **Did you visit** the Louvre? with the short answers *Yes, I did* and *No, I didn't*.

2. Then give each student a holiday card and one of the holiday activity slips at random. If the slip a student gets should by chance describe one of his/her own holiday activities, he/she can tick that activity on his card, but he should keep the slip.

3. Now students begin the milling phase of the activity. The object is to see who can tick all their holiday activities first. Students go around the classroom, meeting in pairs, and question each other about the activities on their small slips: *Did you visit the Eiffel Tower?* for example. Any student who can answer *Yes, I did* can tick that activity on his card.

4. If **one or both** students answered with *yes*, they should **trade slips** after ticking their cards and move on to a new partner. If **neither** can answer with *yes*, they move on to a new partner **without ticking their holiday cards or making a trade.**

5. The first person to finish his holiday by ticking all his activities can sit down. But continue to play until everyone is finished or until you feel the activity has gone on long enough. **Note:** If you take part in the activity, you will be able to monitor the grammar output tactfully.

Extension activity

Ask your class who has actually been to Scotland, Paris, Italy or on a cruise and find out what they did on their holiday. Students could write a short text about a real holiday for their personal *Language Portfolio.*

NEXT A1 Unit 6

Activity 23   What did you do in Paris?   Sheet A

On your last holiday you **went camping in Scotland**.

This is what you did:

You …   … went swimming and fishing in Loch Ness.
         … went to a whisky-tasting event.
         … hiked in the Highlands.
         … listened to bagpipe music.
         … visited Edinburgh.

On your last holiday you **went to Paris for a week**.

This is what you did:

You …   … visited the Eiffel Tower.
         … went shopping in boutiques.
         … had croissants for breakfast.
         … went for a boat ride on the Seine.
         … visited the Louvre Art Museum.

On your last holiday you **went on a cruise**.

This is what you did:

You …   … read in a deck chair.
         … went to the Captain's Dinner.
         … danced in the salon.
         … visited a port.
         … played cards.

On your last holiday you **enjoyed your hobbies in Italy**.

This is what you did:

You …   … learned Italian.
         … drank red wine.
         … did a course in Italian cooking.
         … went shopping for shoes.
         … had cappuccino in a street café.

© 2007 Hueber Verlag · This sheet may be photocopied and used in class.

NEXT A1   Unit 6

Activity 23   What did you do in Paris?   Sheet B

went swimming and fishing in Loch Ness	visited the Eiffel Tower
went to a whisky-tasting event	went shopping in boutiques
hiked in the Highlands	had croissants for breakfast
listened to bagpipe music	went for a boat ride on the Seine
visited Edinburgh	visited the Louvre Art Museum
read in a deck chair	learned Italian
went to the Captain's Dinner	drank red wine
danced in the salon	did a course in Italian cooking
visited a port	went shopping for shoes
played cards	had cappuccino in a street café

NEXT A1 Unit 6

Activity 24 Questions, questions!

Teacher's notes	Activity pairwork, interview, speaking	Focus *wh*-questions with the past simple
15–20 minutes	Aim to find out what students have in common by asking questions	

Preparation

Copy one activity sheet for every two students in your class. Cut the sheets in half along the dotted line.

Procedure

The aim of the activity is to find out what two students have in common by asking *wh*-questions with the past simple.

1. Revise the *wh*-question form with the past simple if necessary.

2. Get students into pairs and give one half of the activity sheet to Partner A and the other half to Partner B.

3. Ask students to look at their questionnaire and tell you what is missing to make each question complete (= *did you*).

4. Ask students first to go through their questionnaires and answer the questions for themselves by writing single words or brief notes in the "Your answer" column.

5. When everyone has finished, students should interview their partner, asking the questions on their questionnaire and noting their partner's answers in the "your partner's answer" column.

6. When the interviews have finished, students should tick the questions where their answers were the same or very similar and add up the total. The pair or pairs with the highest total, i.e. the most things in common, are the "winners". Ask the class for some feedback by finding out which pairs had the most in common and what they had in common.

NEXT A1 Unit 6

Activity 24   Questions, questions!

Partner A

Question	Your answer	Your partner's answer
Where / spend your last holiday?		
What / do on your last birthday?		
When / go to bed last night?		
Where / go to primary school?		
What / have for breakfast today?		
Where / get your English book?		

Partner B

Question	Your answer	Your partner's answer
Where / live 10 years ago?		
When / do your English homework?		
When / get up today?		
When / go on your last holiday?		
What / watch on TV yesterday?		
What / do on your last holiday?		

NEXT A1   Unit 7

Activity 25   Neighbours

Teacher's notes

Activity
pairwork, information gap, writing/speaking

Aim
to describe contrasting pictures in order to make comparative sentences

Focus
describing people
descriptive adjectives
comparative adjective form

Can do
I can describe what other people look like.
I can compare things and people in simple sentences.

20 – 25 minutes

Preparation

Copy one Sheet A and one Sheet B for every two students. Cut the sheets in half along the dotted line.

Procedure

The aim of the activity is for students to describe contrasting pictures to each other in order to formulate comparative questions and answers about the pictures.

1. Review the language for describing people's physical appearance, and the comparative form of adjectives.

2. Hand out the questionnaires and ask students to write the correct comparative form for each question. Check the correct forms together as a class. Then ask students to turn the questionnaires face down on their desks.

3. Get students into pairs. Hand out the Partner A picture to one student and the Partner B picture to the other. Tell students not to show their picture to their partner.

4. Ask students to study their picture for a few moments and prepare to describe it. Students should then begin to describe their picture and the people in it in as much detail as possible, e.g. *There are 5 people in the Jones family. They live in a small house with a small pretty garden. Mr Jones is short, heavy and bald …*

5. When students have finished describing, they should put their pictures face down on the desk. They should now try to answer the questions on the questionnaire together based on what they have heard from each other. If they are not sure of an answer, one of them can look at his/her picture again for help. Students do not need to make full sentence answers at this point.

6. When students have completed their questionnaires, they should look together at each other's pictures to check that they have given the correct answers.

7. Go through the answers with the whole class. Ask your students to give their answers in full sentences.

Key
1. Who has got the bigger house, the Jones family or the Williams family?
   The Williams family *has got the bigger house.*
2. Who has got more comfortable clothes, the Jones family or the Williams family?
   The Jones family *has got more comfortable clothes.*
3. Who has got the more attractive wife, Mr Jones or Mr Williams?
   Mr Williams *has got the more attractive wife.*
4. Who is thinner, Jason Jones or Ted Williams?
   Jason Jones *is thinner than Ted Williams.*
5. Who is taller, Mr Jones or Mr Williams?
   Mr Williams *is taller than Mr Jones.*
6. Who is shorter, Janet Jones or Olivia Williams?
   Janet Jones *is shorter than Olivia Williams.*
7. Who is younger, Johnny or Janet Jones?
   Johnny *is younger than Janet.*
8. Who has got darker hair, Olivia or Ted Williams?
   Ted *has got darker hair than Olivia.*
9. Who has got curlier hair, Mrs Jones or Mrs Williams?
   Mrs Jones *has got curlier hair than Mrs Williams.*
10. Who has got the more expensive car, the Jones family or the Williams family?
    The Williams family *has got the more expensive car.*

NEXT A1   Unit 7

Activity 25   Neighbours   Sheet A

Partner A

This is the Jones family, Mr Jones, Mrs Jones and their children Jason, Janet and baby Johnny.

Partner B

This is the Williams family, Mr Williams, Mrs Williams, and their children Olivia and Ted.

NEXT A1 Unit 7

Activity 25   Neighbours   Sheet B

Question	Answer
1. Who has got the (big) _____ house, the Jones family or the Williams family?	
2. Who has got (comfortable) _____ clothes, the Jones family or the Williams family?	
3. Who has got the (attractive) _____ wife, Mr Jones or Mr Williams?	
4. Who is (thin) _____, Jason Jones or Ted Williams?	
5. Who is (tall) _____, Mr Jones or Mr Williams?	
6. Who is (short) _____, Janet Jones or Olivia Williams?	
7. Who is (young) _____, Johnny or Janet Jones?	
8. Who has got (dark) _____ hair, Olivia or Ted Williams?	
9. Who has got (curly) _____ hair, Mrs Jones or Mrs Williams?	
10. Who has got the (expensive) _____ car, the Jones family or the Williams family?	

✂ -

Question	Answer
1. Who has got the (big) _____ house, the Jones family or the Williams family?	
2. Who has got (comfortable) _____ clothes, the Jones family or the Williams family?	
3. Who has got the (attractive) _____ wife, Mr Jones or Mr Williams?	
4. Who is (thin) _____, Jason Jones or Ted Williams?	
5. Who is (tall) _____, Mr Jones or Mr Williams?	
6. Who is (short) _____, Janet Jones or Olivia Williams?	
7. Who is (young) _____, Johnny or Janet Jones?	
8. Who has got (dark) _____ hair, Olivia or Ted Williams?	
9. Who has got (curly) _____ hair, Mrs Jones or Mrs Williams?	
10. Who has got the (expensive) _____ car, the Jones family or the Williams family?	

NEXT A1 Unit 7

Activity 26   Who's who?

Teacher's notes

Activity
groupwork, information exchange, reading, listening

Focus
family relationships
making comparisons

⏱ 15–20 minutes

Aim
to work out family relationships in family trees

Can do
I can describe family relationships.
I can compare people using simple sentences.

Preparation

Copy one Sheet A for every student in the class. Copy one Sheet B for every 4–5 students and cut out the 15 clue cards. Keep each set of 15 in an envelope or bag.

Procedure

The aim of the activity is to identify the families and family members on Sheet A by listening carefully to the information on the clue cards from Sheet B.

1. Put your students into groups of 4–5. Give each student in the class a copy of Sheet A and each group one set of 15 clue cards.

2. Let the students look at the drawings of the 4 families on Sheet A. Explain that students must try to find out who is who and fill in the 4 family names as well as the first names of each family member. To do so, they must listen carefully to the information on the clue cards.

3. Students should shuffle the clue cards and put them face down in a pile on the desk. They should take turns drawing clue cards and reading them out to the group. If the card gives enough information to identify a person on Sheet A, they should write the name on their sheet and discard the clue card. If not, they should **lay the card in a separate pile for later reference.**

4. Depending on how the cards were shuffled, groups may or may not complete the task after reading each information card once. If they have read all the cards but have not been able to identify every family, they must read the cards they laid aside for future reference once again.
Note: The only way to find out which of the families with two girls and a boy is the Smith family and which is the Gordon family is to listen for the information about which family has a cat!

5. The winner is the first group to completely and correctly label Sheet A. Check by having the students read out the family names and relationships. (For example: *Mr and Mrs Gordon have three children; two girls and a boy. Billy is the middle child. Sally is his older sister and Susie is his younger sister.* Remember that students have not yet learned the superlative form.

Key
Top left box: the Gordon family
– Mr and Mrs Gordon and three children, Sally, Billy and Susie.
– Sally is older than Billy and Susie.
– Billy is older than Susie.

Top right box: the White family
– Ms White and three boys, Christopher, Bobby and Tommy.
– Christopher is older than Bobby and Tommy.
– Tommy is younger than Christopher and Bobby.

Bottom left box: the Miller family
– Mr and Mrs Miller have 4 girls.
– Jane is the baby.
– Ashley and Betsy are the middle children (twins).
– Debby is older than all the other sisters.

Bottom right box: the Smith family
– Mr and Mrs Smith have two girls and a boy just like the Gordons.
– Their boy, Jeffrey, is the middle child, just like in the Gordon family.
– Jessica is his older sister and Judy is his younger sister.
– They have a big black cat.

NEXT A1   Unit 7

Activity 26   Who's who?   Sheet A

The _____ family.

The _____ family.

The _____ family.

The _____ family.

NEXT A1   Unit 7

Activity 26   Who's who?   Sheet B

Mr and Mrs Gordon have two girls and a boy.	Mr and Mrs Smith have two girls and a boy.	Ms White has no husband. She lives alone with her children.
Mr and Mrs Miller have four girls.	The Gordons' son is named Billy. He is older than one sister and younger than the other.	Sally Gordon has a younger sister named Susie Gordon.
Tommy White has two older brothers.	Bobby White is the middle brother. His big brother is Christopher.	Baby Jane Miller has three older sisters.
Debby Miller has a new baby sister.	Ashley and Betsy Miller are the same age. They have two more sisters. One is an older sister and the other is a baby.	Mr and Mrs Smith have a big black cat.
Jeffrey Smith has two sisters. The older sister is Jessica.	Judy Smith has a sister and a brother named Jeffrey. Judy is younger than Jeffrey.	The Smiths' big black cat is called Samantha.

NEXT A1   Unit 8

Activity 27   An ideal place to live

Teacher's notes

Activity
pairwork, guessing game, reading/speaking

Focus
furniture/rooms
describing a person's neighbourhood/area

Aim
to make correct guesses about a partner's home and neighbourhood

Can do
I can describe the area where I live.
I can answer questions and give some simple information about accommodation.

20 minutes

Preparation

Copy one activity sheet for every student in the class.

Procedure

The aim of this activity is for students to try to make correct guesses about a partner's home and neighbourhood.

1. Put students into pairs. Hand out an activity sheet to each student. Ask them first to go through the list of statements and circle or underline one of the options in *italics* in each statement which they think could be true for their partner.

2. When both partners are ready, they should ask each other questions to find out if their guesses were correct, e.g. *Do you live in a city?, Do you have a garden?* etc.

3. If they guessed correctly, they should tick the "my guess was right" column. When they have both interviewed each other, each student should count the number of correct guesses he/she made to find out which of them is the "winner".

4. When everyone has finished, get some feedback from the class by asking the winners of each pair to tell you how many correct guesses they made. You could also ask a few individual students to tell the rest of the class what they found out about their partner, e.g. *Rainer lives in a house in a suburb. He has a garden.* etc.

Extension activity
Students could write a description of their area and their home. This could then form part of their personal *Language Portfolio*.

NEXT A1   Unit 8

Activity 27   An ideal place to live

My partner …	My guess was right.
… lives in a *city/town/suburb/village*.	
… lives in *an apartment/a house*.	
… lives in a *noisy/quiet* place.	
… *has got/hasn't got* a lot of shops in his/her area.	
… lives in *a modern/an old* building.	
… has got *modern/antique* furniture.	
… *has got/hasn't got* a garden.	
… *has got/hasn't got* a big sunny living room.	
… has got *a big TV/a small TV/no TV*.	
… sleeps on *a futon/a water bed/a normal bed*.	
… *has got/hasn't got* a comfortable sofa.	
… *likes/doesn't like* his/her home.	

ID: NEXT A1 Unit 8

Activity 28 Home sweet home

Teacher's notes	Activity pairwork, information gap, speaking	Focus prepositions of place *there is/there are/is there ...?/are there ...?* objects and furniture in a living room
15–20 minutes	Aim to ask about and describe the position of objects and furniture in a room to find the differences	Can do *I can describe where things are in a room.*

Preparation

Copy one activity sheet for every two students. Cut along the dotted line and give one picture to Student A and the other to Student B.

Procedure

The aim of this activity is to find the six differences in the two pictures of a student's room by asking about and describing what is in the room and where the objects are.

1. To lead in to the activity, you may first want to brainstorm furniture and objects which are commonly found in a living room by making a mind-map on the board/OHP. It may also be necessary to revise the following prepositions of place: *behind, between, in, in front of, in the corner of, in the middle of, next to, on, opposite*.

2. Tell students that they have a picture of the same living room, but that there are *six* differences which they have to find.

3. Explain that they should find the differences by asking each other questions based on their own picture using *Is there ...?/Are there ...?* and the short answers *Yes, there is/are./No, there isn't/aren't.*

4. When students find a difference (i.e. when one of them answers a question with *No, there isn't/aren't*), they should say what is in that position in their picture or where the item is, e.g. *There's a telephone on the table* and then **circle it.**

5. After students have found all six differences, they should compare their pictures together to make sure that they have circled the correct differences.

Extension activity: Students could draw a simple sketch of their own living room and write a short description to accompany it. The picture and description could then form part of their personal *Language Portfolio.*

Key (differences)
Picture A:
– the five books on the floor next to the coffee table
– the telephone on the small table next to the sofa
– the tall lamp standing behind the sofa
– the three photos on the wall next to the window
– the large plant in the corner of the room
– the two cushions on the sofa

Picture B:
– the cat on the coffee table
– the lamp on the small table between the sofa and the armchair
– the two posters on the wall next to the door
– the pizza on the desk next to the laptop
– the flowers in a vase on top of the TV
– the jeans on the armchair

NEXT A1   Unit 8

Activity 28   Home sweet home

Picture A

Picture B

NEXT A1   Unit 9

Activity 29   Out on the town!

Teacher's notes	Activity	Focus
	group work, board game, speaking	places of entertainment free time activities
	Aim	**Can do**
20–25 minutes	to try to reach finish first to talk about personal free time activities while moving along a game board	I can say what I do in my free time. I can say what I did in my free time.

Preparation

Make one copy of the board game for every 3 to 5 students in the class. If you have game markers, take one for every student in the class. If you don't, students can organize small objects such as coins, paper clips or erasers to use as markers. You will need one dice for each group, or you could ask students to flip a coin instead of rolling dice – in this case tell them that for heads they move one space and for tails two.

Procedure

The object of the game is to win by reaching FINISH first, after completing speaking tasks along the way.

1. Get students into groups of 3 to 5. Give them a game board, dice and markers, or ask them to find their own markers and use a coin to determine how many squares they should move (see above).

2. Explain that the object of the game is to reach FINISH first. Students should take turns rolling the dice or flipping the coin and moving ahead on the game board. If they land on a space with a speaking task, they should carry it out. If they land on a space with other instructions, they should do as instructed. Make sure that they understand the instructions *Move ahead one space, Move back two spaces,* and *Miss a turn.*

3. As students play, move around the classroom listening in and helping where necessary. You could have small prizes for the winners in each group.

NEXT A1   Unit 9

Activity 29   Out on the town!

OUT ON THE TOWN

START → Move ahead one space. → How often do you eat out? → What kind of coffee do you order at a coffee shop? → Move back two spaces. → What do you like to buy at the shops? → Where do you usually meet your friends? → Miss a turn. → Talk about the last party you went to. → What kinds of sports do you do? → Move ahead one space. → What's your favourite drink at a bar or pub? → Talk about the last concert you went to. → Move back two spaces. → What kinds of museums do you like? → Miss a turn. → How much do you tip at a nice restaurant? → Move ahead one space. → How much free time do you have? → What do you like to eat at your favourite restaurant? → Move back two spaces. → What kinds of films do you like? → Miss a turn. → What did you do last Friday night? → **FINISH**

© 2007 Hueber Verlag · This sheet may be photocopied and used in class.

72

NEXT A1   Unit 9

Activity 30   Well, I never!

Teacher's notes

Activity
group work/whole class, speculating, speaking

Aim
to speculate about activities which the majority of students in the class do
to find out if students individually or groups together make better guesses

Focus
Present simple questions with *Do you ...?*
Present simple questions with *How often ...?*
Questions and answers with *How much/many ...?*
Past simple questions with *Did you ...?*
Adverbs of frequency

Can do
I can say how often I do something.
I can ask about free time activities.
I can say what I normally do in my free time.
I can say what I did in my free time.

20–25 minutes

Preparation

Copy one activity sheet for every group of 4 students. Cut out the statement cards for Groups A, B, C and D and keep each set separate to distribute to each group.

Procedure

The aim of this activity is for students to speculate about activities and facts concerning people in the class and find out if they are true for the majority. They do this first on their own and then together in groups to see if they guess better individually or with others.

1. Get students into groups of 4 as far as possible, although the activity will still work with groups of 3 or 5. Ideally there should be four groups in all. Distribute the group statement cards, making sure that each of the four groups gets a different card (either A, B, C or D) but that each member of the group has the same card as the others in his/her group (all have card A, for example).

2. Tell students that they are going to find out how well they know each other. To do this, they are first going to make guesses about each statement on their own based on what they know about the other students in the class. Then they will discuss their reasons as a group and make a group decision about each statement. Finally they will interview just over half the class to see if the statement is really true or false. They will get a point for each correct guess they make about the class, whether it was an individual or a group guess. The highest score at the end will show them if they guessed better as individuals or as a group.

3. First ask students to read through the statements on their own and decide whether each statement is true or false. Explain that "most of us ..." means more than half of the class, e.g. if your class has 14 students, "most of us" means 8 or more students. They should circle either *True* or *False* for each statement in the column headed **My guess**. Give them only about 1 or 2 minutes to do this.

4. Get students to sit in their groups and to decide together if each statement is true or false. They should circle their choice in the **Group guess** column. Allow them only about 3 or 4 minutes to do this.

5. Ask students to look at each statement and to tell you how they begin the question they need to ask to find out the information. The statements are ordered as follows: (1,2) *Do you ...?*; (3,4) *How much _____ do you ...?*; (5,6) *How many _____ do you ...?*; (7) *How often do you ...?*; (8) *Did you ...?* You may wish to write these on the board/OHP as a support during

NEXT A1 Unit 9

Activity 30 Well, I never!

the activity. Ask students to choose two questions each so that the group covers all the statements, e.g. Student A asks questions for statements 1 and 3, Student B for statements 2 and 4, Student C for statements 5 and 7, and Student D for statements 6 and 8. However the questions are shared amongst the group, encourage students to ask two questions which practise two different tenses/structures.

6. Tell students that they are now going to find out if each statement really is true or false by walking around the classroom interviewing each other. They must make sure that they interview just over half the number of students in the class. Encourage them to interview students in the other groups primarily, but they can also include members of their own group (this will in any case be necessary if you have a smaller class).

7. Once they have interviewed just over half the class, they will be able to circle *True* or *False* in the column headed **Fact**. They should then get back into their groups and share the information they have found out so that they can all complete the **Fact** column.

8. Tell students to compare their individual and group guesses with the real answer (Fact). They should give themselves a tick if their guess was right (and therefore a point), or a cross if it was wrong (and therefore no point) in the ✓/**X** column to the right of **My guess**. They should then do the same with the group guesses and the ✓/**X** column to the right of **Group guess**. The highest point score shows them whether they guessed better as an individual or as a group.

9. You could then ask each group to report back to the rest of the class on which of their statements turned out to be true by reading out the relevant statements from their cards.

NEXT A1   Unit 9

Activity 30   Well, I never!

GROUP A	My guess	✓/ x	Group guess	✓/ x	Fact
1. Most of us go to a gym.	True False		True False		True False
2. Most of us like shopping.	True False		True False		True False
3. Most of us spend more than 70 euros on food shopping every week.	True False		True False		True False
4. Most of us have more than 50 euros with us this evening.	True False		True False		True False
5. Most of us go on more than one holiday a year.	True False		True False		True False
6. Most of us have more than one free day a week.	True False		True False		True False
7. Most of us go to the cinema twice a month.	True False		True False		True False
8. Most of us went out with friends last weekend.	True False		True False		True False

✂

GROUP B	My guess	✓/ x	Group guess	✓/ x	Fact
1. Most of us play computer games.	True False		True False		True False
2. Most of us like football.	True False		True False		True False
3. Most of us spend more than 30 euros at restaurants every week.	True False		True False		True False
4. Most of us have more than 20 euros with us this evening.	True False		True False		True False
5. Most of us watch more than three hours of TV a day.	True False		True False		True False
6. Most of us have more than two hobbies.	True False		True False		True False
7. Most of us go out with friends more than twice a week.	True False		True False		True False
8. Most of us spent more than 20 euros in a bar last week.	True False		True False		True False

© 2007 Hueber Verlag · This sheet may be photocopied and used in class.

NEXT A1 Unit 9

Activity 30 Well, I never!

GROUP C	My guess	✓/x	Group guess	✓/x	Fact
1. Most of us listen to music on the way to work.	True False		True False		True False
2. Most of us go to after-work parties.	True False		True False		True False
3. Most of us spend more than 50 euros on books every month.	True False		True False		True False
4. Most of us have more than 100 euros with us this evening.	True False		True False		True False
5. Most of us spend more than two hours a day on sports.	True False		True False		True False
6. Most of us have more than four bars in the street where we live.	True False		True False		True False
7. Most of us go to a music concert more than twice a year.	True False		True False		True False
8. Most of us went to a disco last weekend.	True False		True False		True False

---

GROUP D	My guess	✓/x	Group guess	✓/x	Fact
1. Most of us go shopping with friends.	True False		True False		True False
2. Most of us like dancing.	True False		True False		True False
3. Most of us spend more than 15 euros on newspapers and magazines every week.	True False		True False		True False
4. Most of us have more than 70 euros with us this evening.	True False		True False		True False
5. Most of us do more than two hours of sport every week.	True False		True False		True False
6. Most of us have more than twenty music CDs.	True False		True False		True False
7. Most of us go to a bar more than three times a week.	True False		True False		True False
8. Most of us spent more than eight hours at work today.	True False		True False		True False

NEXT A1 Unit 10

Activity 31 Getting there

Teacher's notes

Activity
group work, game, vocabulary

Aim
to win a word game by finding original answers

Focus
types of transport
descriptive adjectives

15–20 minutes

Preparation

Copy the activity sheet for every 2 groups of 4 to 5 students. Cut along the dotted line.

Procedure

The aim of the game is for students to find types of transport in each descriptive category that are as original as possible while still being valid types of transport somewhere in the world. As various answers are possible, you will have to decide if a team's answer is acceptable or not. If they are challenged, teams should try to justify their answers in English. But don't be too strict. The activity is meant to provide spontaneous, enjoyable interaction with vocabulary, both old and new, and to encourage students to discover the fun of working with words.

1. Ask students to form teams of 4 to 5. Give each team an activity sheet and ask them to write a team name at the top.

2. Explain to students that they should think of as original a type of transport as possible for each statement. Emphasize that the type of transport must be a real form of transport somewhere in the world. Tell students to discuss each statement quietly and agree on an answer. You may need to help students with vocabulary or let them use dictionaries.

3. Set a maximum time limit of 10 minutes for groups to write their answers. Then stop the activity and ask groups to swap papers.

4. Go through teams' answers point by point by asking each team to read aloud the answer they have on the sheet in front of them. Teams score a point only if their answer is completely original, i.e. if they are the only team to have written the type of transport. You should reject an answer only if you feel it is not a valid type of transport or does not fit with the descriptive adjective in the sentence.

5. The group which scores the most points is the winner.

Examples for possible "original" answers:
1. hot air balloon
2. racing car
3. cruise ship
4. rickshaw
5. rocket ship
6. bicycle
7. camel
8. ship
9. tractor
10. rollerblades

NEXT A1 Unit 10

Activity 31   Getting there

Name a **dangerous** type of transport. _____

Name a **fast** type of transport. _____

Name an **expensive** type of transport. _____

Name an **exciting** type of transport. _____

Name a **modern** type of transport. _____

Name a **cheap** type of transport. _____

Name a **slow** type of transport. _____

Name a **relaxing** type of transport. _____

Name a **safe** type of transport. _____

Name your group's **favourite** type of transport. _____

Total points: _____

Name a **dangerous** type of transport. _____

Name a **fast** type of transport. _____

Name an **expensive** type of transport. _____

Name an **exciting** type of transport. _____

Name a **modern** type of transport. _____

Name a **cheap** type of transport. _____

Name a **slow** type of transport. _____

Name a **relaxing** type of transport. _____

Name a **safe** type of transport. _____

Name your group's **favourite** type of transport. _____

Total points: _____

© 2007 Hueber Verlag · This sheet may be photocopied and used in class.

NEXT A1   Unit 10

Activity 32   Out and about

Teacher's notes	Activity	Focus
15–20 minutes	pairwork, dictation, speaking	giving directions buildings in a town
	Aim to give and understand spoken directions	**Can do** I can give and understand simple directions.

Preparation

Copy one activity sheet for every 2 students in your class. Cut along the dotted line and distribute the Student A map to one student and the Student B map to the other.

Procedure

The aim of this activity is for students to ask for and give directions to different places in a town orally to find out where certain buildings are.

1. Tell students that they are going to ask each other how to get to the different places stated under their map and give directions to the places that their partner asks for. Explain that Student A starts each time from the Tourist Information Centre and Student B from Bill's Bar.

2. If necessary, write the question *How do I get to …?* on the board/OHP to remind students how to ask for directions to each building on their list. Before students start, you may also wish to revise the phrases for giving directions – *walk down _____ Street/Road, turn left/right, walk past _____, it's on the left/right.*

With a more able class, you could also encourage students to use prepositions to describe exactly where each building is, e.g. *next to, between, opposite,* etc.

3. Ask students not to show their maps to their partner while they are doing the activity. They should listen to where their partner wants to go and describe the simplest way to get there. When they have finished describing, their partner should **mark where each building is on his/her map.**

4. After students have completed the activity, they should show each other their maps and compare where each building is to make sure that they have given and/or followed the directions correctly.

NEXT A1   Unit 10

Activity 32   Out and about

Student A

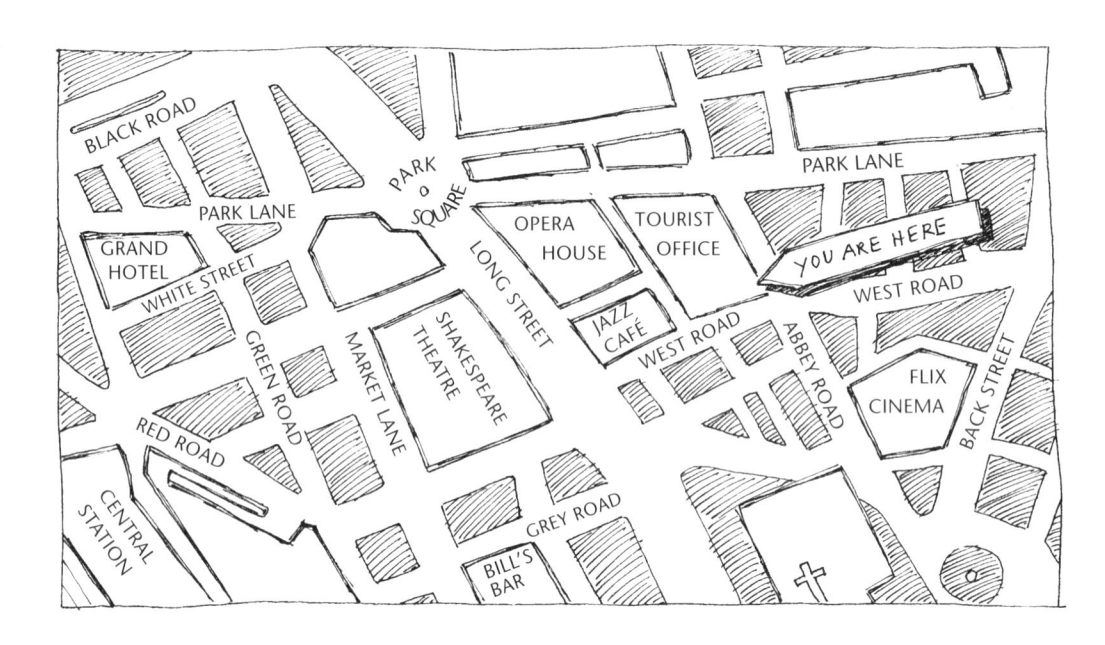

You are at the Tourist Office. Ask your partner how to get to:

- the Town Hall
- the City Museum
- the university
- the bus station
- St. John's Cathedral
- Paddy's Bar

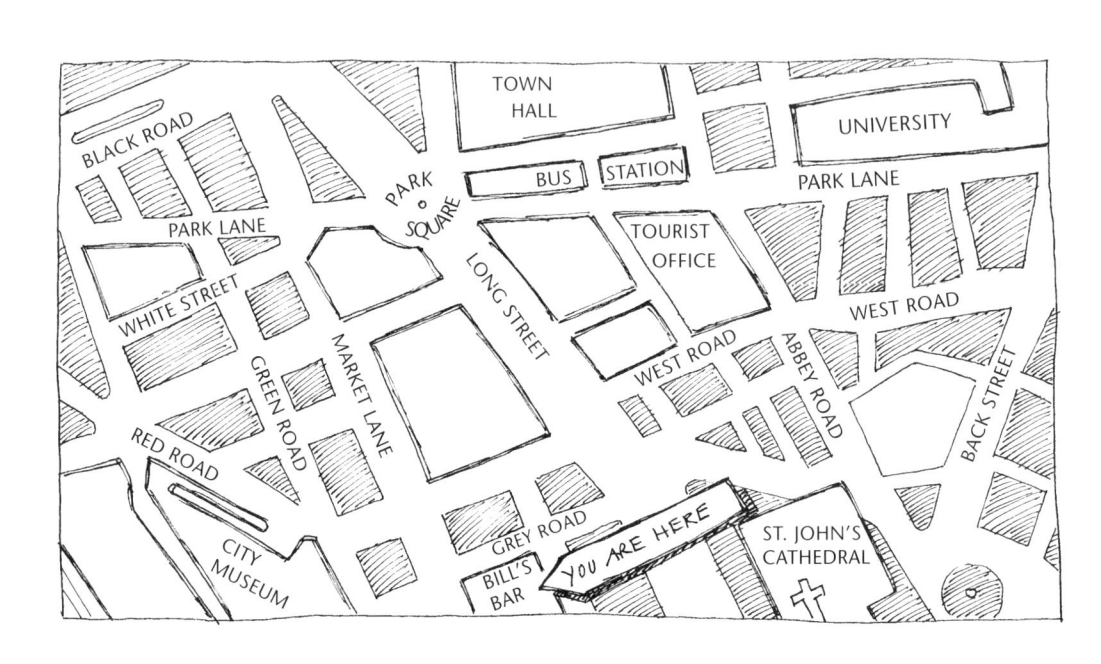

Student B

You are at Bill's Bar. Ask your partner how to get to:

- Central Station
- the Flix Cinema
- the Shakespeare Theatre
- the Jazz Café
- the Grand Hotel
- the Opera House

© 2007 Hueber Verlag · This sheet may be photocopied and used in class.

NEXT A1   Unit 11

Activity 33   Let's go out

Teacher's notes

Activity
whole class, interview, speaking

Aim
to find partners for free time activities

25 – 30 minutes

Focus
making suggestions and arrangements
accepting and declining invitations

Can do
I can make suggestions for going out.

Preparation

Copy the activity sheet so that there are enough diary cards for each student in the class and at least four programmes. Cut out the diary cards and give one to each student. Stick the programmes on the walls in different places around the classroom.

Procedure

This extended activity provides students with practice of making suggestions and arrangements in a realistic context. The aim is for students to arrange to meet a different student to go to a different free time activity each day. The task is made more challenging because the four activities on the programme are not available every day. Students should first use the programmes to arrange four activities on four days. This will leave one day free, on which they should think of another activity they want to do and find another student to do this with.

1. If necessary, review the language of suggesting to meet (*Let's … / Why don't we …? / What are you doing on …?*) and accepting or declining invitations. (*Sure, I'd love to. / That's a good idea. / Nothing special. / I'm afraid I can't … / I'd love to, but … / Sorry, but I can't …*).

2. Explain to students that they have a week's holiday and that they want to do something different on each day with a different person in the class. On four of their free days, they want to go to one of the concerts or performances listed in the programmes stuck on the walls and on the fifth free day they can think of any other free time activity that they want to do. Emphasize to students that they should first arrange to do the four activities from the programme, and then think of a fifth activity for the free day which is left over and try to find another student to do it with.

3. Tell students first to look at the programmes to see the options there are for four of their free days. They should then walk around the classroom, asking other students what they are doing on certain days (*What are you doing on Monday?*) and suggesting activities (*Let's go to a concert*).

4. When they find another student who is free on a day when they are also free, they should both go together to one of the programmes and decide what they want to do (*Why don't we …?*), bearing in mind that they can't do something which they have already arranged to do with another student. Once they have arranged to do something together, they should write down the student's name and what they have decided to do next to the corresponding day on their diary card, and move on.

5. If students can't do something on the day suggested or have already arranged to do the suggested activity with another student, they should decline the invitation and say what they are doing on that day, e.g. *I'd love to, but I'm going to the cinema with Tobias on Tuesday.* They can then suggest doing something on one of the days they still have free or suggest a different activity, e.g. *What are you doing on Monday? Why don't we go to the theatre?*

6. Students continue the procedure until they have arranged to do four different activities with four different students. They should then think of another free time activity they want to do on their fifth free day and try to find a student who is free on the same day and wants to do the activity with them.

7. Allow students about 20 minutes to complete their diaries, then stop the activity and ask them to sit down. Ask a couple of individual students to tell the rest of the class what they are doing in their free week.

NEXT A1   Unit 11

Activity 33   Let's go out

Diaries

Monday _____	Monday _____
Tuesday _____	Tuesday _____
Wednesday _____	Wednesday _____
Thursday _____	Thursday _____
Friday _____	Friday _____

Monday _____	Monday _____
Tuesday _____	Tuesday _____
Wednesday _____	Wednesday _____
Thursday _____	Thursday _____
Friday _____	Friday _____

Monday _____	Monday _____
Tuesday _____	Tuesday _____
Wednesday _____	Wednesday _____
Thursday _____	Thursday _____
Friday _____	Friday _____

PROGRAMME   TIPS OF THE WEEK

_____THE OLDIE CINEMA _____

Casablanca The classic film starring Humphrey Bogart and Ingrid Bergman.

Performance times
Monday   2.15 p.m., 6.30 p.m.
Tuesday   7.45 p.m.
Wednesday   7.45 p.m.
Friday   10 p.m.

_____THE PRINCE'S THEATRE_____

Hamlet Shakespeare's tragedy in a new version by the Royal Shakespeare Company.

Performance times
Tuesday   8 p.m.
Wednesday   8 p.m.
Thursday   8 p.m.

_____THE ROYAL OPERA HOUSE_____

Cosi fan tutti A new performance of the opera by Wolfgang Amadeus Mozart.

Performance times
Monday   7.30 p.m.
Wednesday   7.30 p.m.
Thursday   3 p.m., 8 p.m.
Friday   7.30 p.m.

_____CITY CONCERT HALL_____

Cool Britannia The world famous BritPop band live.

Performance times
Thursday   8.30 p.m.
Friday   8.30 p.m.

© 2007 Hueber Verlag · This sheet may be photocopied and used in class.

NEXT A1 Unit 11

Activity 34   What are you doing on Friday night?

Teacher's notes

Activity
whole class, role play, speaking

Aim
to compare what people usually do at the weekend with fictitious plans

Focus
present continuous for the future
fixed arrangements
routine activities (present simple)

Can do
I can name some things people do after work.
I can ask and talk about other people's plans.

20–25 minutes

Preparation

Copy one Sheet A for each student in your class and one Sheet B for every 12 students. Cut each Sheet B into 12 horizontal strips by cutting along the horizontal lines. If you have more than 12 students, use duplicate texts.

Procedure

The aim of the activity is for students to complete a table by finding out about activities other students usually do and their fictitious plans for the weekend.

1. You may first want to review the present continuous for fixed arrangements if necessary. Then give every student in the class a strip of paper from Sheet B and ask them to fill in the left-hand side of their strip with one activity that they typically do on a Friday night. Explain that the other piece of information already on the card is what they are doing this Friday.

2. Hand out a *Find someone who …* sheet to each student and explain that they must complete the table with information from other students in the class.

They should do this by moving around the classroom, first asking each other *What are you doing this Friday?* to find the relevant sentence in the table on Sheet A and then asking *What do you usually do on Friday night?* to find out what the student usually does.

3. Allow students enough time to complete their table, then get them to sit down. Ask a few individual students to report back to the class on what they found out by making contrasting sentences. As an example, write on the board/OHP: *Susanne usually watches TV on Friday night, but this Friday she is going to the circus with her children.*

NEXT A1   Unit 11

Activity 34   What are you doing on Friday night?   Sheet A

Find someone who is …	Name:	What he/she usually does:
going to a pop concert.		
meeting friends at a beer garden.		
leaving for a Rhine boat trip.		
watching a football game.		
going to a Mozart opera.		
going to his/her first Japanese lesson.		
going to an art show.		
going to the circus with his/her children.		
having dinner at a 5-star restaurant.		
playing the saxophone at a jazz club.		
going to a Salsa club to dance.		
flying to London for the weekend.		

© 2007 Hueber Verlag · This sheet may be photocopied and used in class.

NEXT A1   Unit 11

Activity 34   What are you doing on Friday night?   Sheet B

Usually do:	**This Friday night:** go to a pop concert
Usually do:	**This Friday night:** meet friends at a beer garden
Usually do:	**This Friday night:** leave for a Rhine boat trip
Usually do:	**This Friday night:** watch a football game
Usually do:	**This Friday night:** go to a Mozart opera
Usually do:	**This Friday night:** go to your first Japanese lesson
Usually do:	**This Friday night:** go to an art show
Usually do:	**This Friday night:** go to the circus with your children
Usually do:	**This Friday night:** have dinner at a 5-star restaurant
Usually do:	**This Friday night:** play saxophone at a jazz club
Usually do:	**This Friday night:** go to a Salsa club to dance
Usually do:	**This Friday night:** fly to London for the weekend

© 2007 Hueber Verlag · This sheet may be photocopied and used in class.

NEXT A1   Unit 12

Activity 35   Body and Soul Bingo

Teacher's notes

Activity
whole class, game, vocabulary

Focus
health, illness
the body

Aim
to win a Bingo game by matching words with their definitions

15 minutes

Preparation

For a class of up to 16 students, make one copy each of Sheets A and B. If you have more than 16 students, make one more copy of Sheet A and use a few duplicate bingo sheets. Cut out each of the 8 bingo word cards. For yourself, make a copy of the words and definitions you will need for the game (see below).

Procedure

This activity is based on the well-known game *Bingo*. The object of the game is to cross off all the words on a bingo card by matching them with their definitions, which the teacher will read out.

1. Tell the class that you are going to review the vocabulary of the unit with a word game. Distribute a bingo word card to each student.

2. Explain the rules of the game. You are going to read out the definitions of certain words from the unit, one at a time. Students must identify the word being defined and cross it off if it is on their word card **(20 words will be dictated but only 9 of them are on each card)**.

3. Explain that there will be two parts to the game and two winners in this order: (1) the first student who crosses off **three words in a row in any direction** (horizontally, vertically or diagonally) and calls out *Line!*; (2) the first student who crosses off **all the words on the card** and calls out *Bingo!* Each time, check that students have crossed off the correct words by asking them to read out the items that they have crossed off. If they are all words that you have already read out, the student has won. **Note:** If you have used duplicate cards, there may be more than one winner at a time.

4. You can read out the 20 words (listed on page 87) in any order. You should mark off the definitions as you read them out to keep track of which ones you have already done.

Extension activity
Ask students to work in pairs and to look through the coursebook and select 4 or 5 words which they can define clearly and simply. Give them a few minutes to select the words, then ask them to write short, simple definitions. Allow them enough time to write the definitions, then ask them to join another pair. They should then read out their definitions to each other and guess what the word is.

NEXT A1   Unit 12

Activity 35   Body and Soul Bingo

Bingo definitions

(You can read the definitions out in any order, but don't read the words in brackets! Tick off the words as you dictate their definitions.)

(nose):	You breathe with this part of your body.	(doctor):	This is someone who helps you when you are ill.
(mouth):	You eat and speak with this part of your body.	(fruit):	This food is sweet and healthy.
(eyes):	You see with this part of your body.	(fast food):	These are unhealthy foods like hamburgers and pizza.
(head):	Your eyes, nose and mouth are on this part of your body.	(stress):	This is what we feel when we have too much work and not enough relaxation.
(knees):	They are in the middle of your legs and you can bend them.	(hobby):	This is something we like to do in our free time.
(ears):	You hear with this part of your body.	(hospital):	This is a place where you can stay when you are very ill.
(headache):	You have this when your head hurts.	(aspirin):	This is a pill you can take when you don't feel well.
(sore throat):	You have this when your throat hurts.	(vegetable):	This is a healthy food like a carrot or broccoli.
(lifestyle):	This is how you live; the kind of life you have.	(check-up):	The doctor gives you this to see if you are healthy.
(healthy):	This is the opposite of unhealthy.		
(non-smoker):	This is what we call a person who is not a smoker.		

NEXT A1   Unit 12

Activity 35   Body and Soul Bingo   Sheet A

nose	hobby	knees
headache	lifestyle	non-smoker
fruit	stress	sore throat

headache	nose	stress
fruit	eyes	hobby
vegetable	hospital	non-smoker

mouth	head	doctor
sore throat	healthy	ears
hospital	hobby	aspirin

sore throat	fast food	mouth
check-up	healthy	doctor
hobby	head	aspirin

fruit	stress	nose
vegetable	eyes	hospital
healthy	headache	lifestyle

sore throat	healthy	mouth
doctor	fast food	aspirin
check-up	hobby	head

doctor	fast food	hobby
head	check-up	ears
aspirin	sore throat	mouth

vegetable	nose	lifestyle
non-smoker	knees	mouth
headache	head	eyes

© 2007 Hueber Verlag · This sheet may be photocopied and used in class.

NEXT A1   Unit 12

Activity 35   Body and Soul Bingo   Sheet B

aspirin	check-up	mouth
eyes	head	sore throat
ears	knees	headache

nose	fruit	healthy
non-smoker	stress	vegetable
ears	eyes	hospital

healthy	knees	hospital
vegetable	non-smoker	fruit
stress	nose	fast food

vegetable	hobby	stress
healthy	ears	check-up
lifestyle	aspirin	headache

non-smoker	hobby	vegetable
lifestyle	doctor	knees
hospital	nose	fast food

check-up	healthy	aspirin
knees	doctor	fast food
non-smoker	fruit	hospital

eyes	sore throat	non-smoker
doctor	ears	fruit
stress	lifestyle	headache

non-smoker	ears	lifestyle
hobby	check-up	nose
headache	fruit	healthy

© 2007 Hueber Verlag · This sheet may be photocopied and used in class.

NEXT A1   Unit 12

Activity 36   A healthy life

Teacher's notes

Activity
whole class, interview, speaking

Focus
healthy lifestyle

⏱ 15 – 20 minutes

Aim
to find "kindred spirits" who have ticked the same answers on a checklist

Can do
I can say how often I do things.

Preparation

Copy one activity sheet for every student in the class.

Procedure

The aim of the activity is for students to find other students in the class who have a similar lifestyle (i.e. who have ticked the same statements on the worksheet as being true or false for them).

1. Hand out the activity sheet to your students. Ask them to go through the list of statements and tick the true or false column, depending on their lifestyles.

2. At this stage you shouldn't need to practise the question form with *do you*. But point out that it is awkward to ask questions in the negative. For statements 5, 6, and 10 on the activity sheet, ask students to suggest other ways of getting the information they want, e.g. by making a positive question such as ***Do you eat fast food?***

3. Now ask students to walk around the classroom and interview fellow students individually, asking questions with *do*, e.g *Do you do sports once or twice a week?* They should ask each other one question before moving on to another student.

If both students answer the question the same way (whether with *yes* or with *no*), they should write each other's names in the third column. You might want to write the phrases *So do I / Neither do I* on the board/OHP so that students can express their similarities.

4. When most students have finished, or when you feel the activity has lasted long enough, get students to sit down and ask a few individual students to report back, e.g. *Michael and I do sports once or twice a week*, etc. You could then also ask for a few more details, e.g. *Which sports do you do?* etc.

5. You could find out who ticked the most statements as true (first answer column) and award them a prize for having the healthiest lifestyle.

Extension activity
Students could write a brief text about their lifestyle with a few sentences about their healthy habits and some describing their less healthy habits. This could be put in their personal ***Language Portfolio.***

NEXT A1 Unit 12

Activity 36   A healthy life

Do you have a healthy lifestyle?	True for me	False for me	Partner with same answer (name)
I do sports once or twice a week.			
I sometimes walk or ride my bike to work.			
I eat fruit and vegetables every day.			
I eat fish once or twice a week.			
I never eat fast food.			
I don't smoke and I don't live with a smoker.			
I relax in the evenings and at weekends.			
I have a hobby that I love.			
I often go out with my friends.			
I don't feel stressed very often.			
I do yoga once or twice a week.			
I go to the doctor for a check-up every year.			

NEXT

FLEXTRAS

This section provides *flexible, extra* suggestions for activities which can be used to practise various aspects of English in a fun way if you want to "warm students up" at the beginning of a lesson, provide a little light relief during the lesson, or if you find that you have some time left over at the end of a lesson. They can all be carried out in approximately 5–10 minutes and require little or no preparation. With many of the activities, you are free to decide which vocabulary or grammar you want students to practise and how much time you wish to spend on them.

Note: The activities marked with an asterisk (*) require a small, soft ball for students to throw to each other.

All mixed up

Choose 5 words from the previous unit(s) and write them as anagrams on the board/OHP, e.g. for the word *football,* you could write *lbaofolt.* Ask students to work out the word from the anagram, and as soon as they know the word, they should come to the board/OHP and write the correct word next to the corresponding anagram. Students could then repeat the procedure by choosing one familiar word and writing it as an anagram on the board/OHP for the others in the class to work out.

Alphaball*

Get students to sit in a circle. There are two possible variations: (1) Say a letter of the alphabet, e.g. *s.* Throw the ball to a student and elicit the next letter in the alphabet, e.g. *t.* (2) Elicit the two letters before and after the letter, e.g. *r* and *t.* The student with the ball then does the same with a different letter.

Categories

This game is similar to the German parlour game *Stadt, Land, Fluss,* which most students will be familiar with. It can be used for any vocabulary fields which you wish to revise. Think of four categories which correspond to vocabulary fields which students have covered sufficiently, e.g. *Nationalities, Food and drink, Free-time activities, Buildings.* Ask students to write a table with four columns headed with these categories. Get them into groups of 4 or 5. Each student should take it in turn to say the alphabet silently to themselves in English and one other student in the group should say "Stop" at any point they wish. The student who ran through the alphabet silently then tells the others the letter they stopped at. Students should then complete the columns with one word which begins with the letter and matches each category as fast as possible, e.g. for *s: Swiss, soup, swimming, supermarket.* As soon as a student has completed all four categories, he/she shouts "stop!" and the others must stop as well, even if they haven't completed their tables. The fastest student should read aloud their words for each category. Each student then gets a point for every word which he/she has written down in each category which no other student in their group has written down. The student who has most points at the end is the winner.

Definitions

Give a slip of paper to each student. Ask them to write a word they have learnt from the previous unit(s). Tell them to swap papers with another student. The student looks at the word and writes a short, simple definition of the word on the back of the piece of paper. Students swap papers again, but with a different student. The student should read the definition and guess the word. If students can't guess the word because the definition is unclear, ask them to suggest an alternative, clearer definition.

Give me a break!

This is a variation of the game "Simon says". Lead a short "fitness routine" to allow students to move around and rest their brains for a moment. Ask students to stand up and tell them to follow your instructions, but only if you say "Class, …" at the beginning of each instruction. If you don't, they shouldn't move. Any student who moves after an instruction without "Class, …" at the beginning must sit down and is out of the game. The last student(s) standing is (are) the winner(s). Possible instructions include: *sit down, stand up, touch your knees, open your book, go to the window, open the window, close your eyes, go to your desk,* etc. You could then get a couple of individual students to lead the "fitness routine" themselves following the same procedure.

Hangman

Write the letters of a familiar word as lines on the board/ OHP, e.g. *restaurant* as _ _ _ _ _ _ _ _ _ _. Ask students to call out letters of the alphabet individually. Write in any letters which are in the word. If the letters called out are not in the word, draw one step of the hangman picture. The complete picture looks like this:

If students guess the word before the hangman picture is complete, they have won. They have 10 wrong guesses before they lose. They may call out the word as soon as they think they know it. If it is the wrong word, add to the hangman picture. Ask the winning student to think of or find a word in his/her coursebook which they have all learnt and to come up to the board/OHP and write it as lines, following your example. The student should then ask the other students to call out letters of the alphabet individually and follow the procedure described above.

I can see it

This activity is a guessing game based on *I spy*. Choose an object that you can see in the classroom. Say "I see something in the classroom that begins with the letter (B)". Students must ask questions that can only be answered with *yes* or *no* to guess the object that you have in mind. Encourage students to ask for more information with simple questions, e.g. *Is it red? Is it on a desk/on the wall?*, etc. However, they can also simply ask *Is it a book? Is it the board?* etc. You could then get students into groups to play the game amongst themselves.

In top form!*

This activity can be used in a variety of ways. Two possible examples are: (1) opposites; (2) verb form practice. Get students to sit in a circle. (1) With adjective opposites, say an adjective, e.g. *cheap,* throw the ball to a student and elicit the opposite, e.g. *expensive*. The student with the ball then does the same with a different adjective. (2) Say a verb in the infinitive form, e.g. *say*. Throw the ball to a student and elicit the past simple form, e.g. *said*. The student with the ball then does the same with a different verb, and the procedure is repeated.

Noughts and Crosses

Divide the class into two teams. One team (Team A) is noughts (0) and the other (Team B) is crosses (X). Draw the noughts and crosses grid on the board with 9 equally-spaced fields like this:

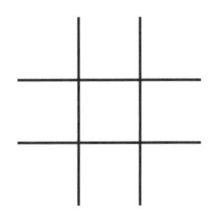

Begin by asking a member of Team A a question. The questions can cover any topic you like; they can be grammar or vocabulary questions or comprehension questions about a text the class has just read, and so on. If the student answers the question correctly, Team A can choose any of the nine spaces on the board for their nought, which you should then draw on the grid. If the student answers incorrectly, don't draw anything on the grid and move on to Team B. Do the same with a student from Team B. If the question is answered correctly, Team B can tell you where they want you to put their cross. Each time a team has a turn, a different member of the team should answer the question. The game ends when either Team A or Team B has three noughts or three crosses in a row on the grid, either horizontally, vertically or diagonally. Here is one example:

X	0	
X	X	X
0		0

Packing a suitcase

This activity is based on the German *Ich packe meinen Koffer und nehme … mit,* which most students will know. Explain to students that they must help you decide what to put in a suitcase for a holiday. Begin by saying "In my suitcase there is a pullover". Then ask a student to continue. He/she must repeat what you said and add something to the suitcase, e.g. *In my suitcase there is a pullover and a pair of jeans*. The next student repeats what is already in the suitcase and adds another item, and so on, with students taking it in turns to add items to the suitcase. Continue until students are unable to remember or you think the activity has lasted long enough.

Other possible topics include: "Daily routine activities" (*Every day, I …,* to practise the present simple), "What I did last weekend" (*Last weekend I …,* to practise the past simple), "What I had for breakfast" (*For breakfast today, I had …* to practise *a* and *some*), etc.

Picture it!

Students should think of an object that they all know the English for and that they can draw. Get students into groups of 4 or 6. Give them a piece of paper each. Ask one student in the group to time the activity – students have *one minute* to draw their object. Two variations of this activity are possible: (1) Each student draws his/her picture silently within the time limit. The others in the group watch what is being drawn and can guess

NEXT FLEXTRAS

what the object is as soon as they think they recognise it by asking *Is it a/an …?* The first student in the group to guess what the object is correctly gets a point. The winner is the student who has most points at the end of the activity. (2) Students work with a partner, i.e. in a group of 4 or 6, there will be 2 or 3 pairs respectively. One student from one pair draws his/her picture silently within the time limit. The other pair monitors the time. His/her partner has one minute to guess what the object is. If he/she guesses the object within the time limit, the pair wins a point. If not, the other pair wins the point and has the chance to win a bonus point if they guess the object correctly.

Questions, questions, questions*

Get students to sit in a circle. Ask a question, e.g. *Where do you come from?, What did you do at the weekend?* etc., depending on the grammar which students have practised in the coursebook. Throw the ball to a student and get him/her to answer. If the student makes a mistake with the tense, ask the others in the group to correct. The student with the ball then thinks of another question, says it aloud and throws the ball to another student and the activity continues. The further on in the course you are, the more you should encourage students to mix the tenses they use.

Schlopp

Think of a verb, e.g. *swim*. Tell the class that you are thinking of a verb and they must try to guess it within a certain time limit. To do so, they must ask questions using the word *schlopp* to substitute for the verb they are trying to guess. Encourage a variety of questions, e.g. *Can you schlopp? Can most of us schlopp? Do we schlopp at work/in class/at home? Do we schlopp in summer/winter? Did you schlopp yesterday? Did you schlopp on holiday?* The game is over when the word has been guessed or the time limit is up.

Sentence building*

Get students to sit in a circle. Start a sentence, e.g. with the word *he*. Throw the ball to a student. Elicit any word which can come after the word you said which makes sense, e.g. *went*. The student with the ball then throws the ball to another student and he/she must continue the sentence with the next word, e.g. *to*. Once a complete sentence is arrived at, the next student with the ball can start a new one. The procedure is then repeated.

Talk about it!

At the beginning of a lesson, ask pairs to talk to each other about a specific topic for about 5 minutes. You could either specify the topic yourself or give students the freedom to talk about whatever they want. The topic could be based on their last lesson, but any topic which they can discuss is possible, e.g. what they like doing, what they did at the weekend, the last party they went to, the last film they saw or book they read, etc. Encourage them to have a natural, spontaneous and authentic conversation, talking to each other, asking questions, and so on.

Teacher, tell us!

Choose a topic you are willing to answer questions about and tell students what it is, e.g. *eating habits*. They must ask questions that can be answered with *yes* or *no*, e.g. *Do you eat breakfast? Do you like muesli? Do you snack between meals?* etc. To practise the past simple, choose a topic like "My last weekend" or "My summer holiday". Every time you can answer with *yes*, the class gets a point, but if your answer is *no*, you get a point. The game is over when either you or the class has 10 points.

Tell the truth!

Ask everyone in the class to stand up. Depending on what tense or vocabulary you want to practise, say sentences like the following: (present simple) *You can sit down if you get up before seven. You can sit down if you eat muesli for breakfast. You can sit down if you go to work at 8 o'clock;* or (past simple) *You can sit down if you read the newspaper yesterday. You can sit down if you watched TV yesterday. You can sit down if you finished work before 6 p.m. yesterday,* and so on. Students may only sit down if the sentence is true for them. Continue until the whole class is seated again.

What time is it?

Draw two round clocks on the board without the hour and minute hands. Form two teams with your class. The first two players, one from each team, come to the board. Call out a time. Both students must draw the hands of their clock so that they show the right time. The first one to finish and have the correct time wins a point for their team. Follow the same procedure with the other team members. The team with the most points at the end is winner.

NEXT FLEXTRAS

Who am I?

Explain that the object of the game is to guess the famous person you are thinking of. Think of a famous person and tell the class whether this person is alive or dead. Students take turns asking you questions that can be answered only with *yes* and *no*, e.g. (for someone who is alive using the present simple) *Is it a man? Is he a singer? Does he live in Europe?*, or (for someone who is dead using the past simple) *Did she live in Egypt? Was she a Queen?* Give the class a 5-minute time limit or a maximum of 20 questions.

A variation of this activity is to cut up small pieces of paper (about 6cm x 6cm), give one piece to each student and ask them to write the name of a famous person, alive or dead, on it, but not to show anyone. While students are thinking of a famous person, give each of them a small piece of Sellotape and ask them to stick it down on the side on which they have written so that part of it juts out over the piece of paper. When they have written a name, they should find another student in the class and stick their piece of paper onto his/her forehead without letting them see the name on the piece of paper. Ask students to get into groups of 4–6 and to ask each other *yes/no* questions in the first person (*Am I …?/Do I …?/Was I …?/Did I …?*). They may ask as many questions as they like until they get a negative answer, when play moves on to the next student, who follows the same procedure. The winner is the first student in the group to guess the famous person on his/her forehead.

Word Bingo

Choose a vocabulary field from the unit you are working on such as *fruit and vegetables, free-time activities or methods of transport*. Ask students to draw a nine square bingo grid on a piece of paper and then look at the unit in their coursebooks and choose nine words from this vocabulary field to put in their grid. For example:

lemon	grape	mushroom
apple	banana	grapefruit
broccoli	carrot	onion

Using the coursebook unit so that you cover all the possibilities, call out the German translation of the words from the vocabulary field one by one. Students cross off the English equivalent if they have it on their grid. The first student to cross off all nine words calls out *Bingo!* and is the winner.

Word King

Choose vocabulary from a recent unit that you want to revise. Get the class to stand up. Read out a word or phrase in German to a pair of students (i.e. two students standing next to each other). They must give the correct English version as quickly as possible. The student who is slower sits down. Follow the same procedure with new words and each different pair in the class until finally only half the class remains standing. Give these students a new partner and a new word or phrase to say in English. Continue until there is only one person left standing. He/she is the word king!

Word Snake*

Get students to sit in a circle in the middle of the classroom. Begin by saying a word which students are familiar with and then throw a soft ball to a student who must now say a word starting with the letter your word ended with. This student then throws the ball to another student, who must again think of a word starting with the letter that the preceding word ended with, and so on. This is a fun way to revise all kinds of vocabulary.